Teach Social Media
A Plan for Creating a Course Your Students Will Love

Matthew J. Kushin, Ph.D.

Build 1-2p

Book jacket designed by Brad Hamann from bradhamanndesign.com
Page layout by Matthew J. Kushin
Editing assistance by Masahiro Yamamoto, Francis Dalisay, Kelin Kushin and Trish Kushin.

To my 11th grade English and History teachers, Mrs. Segal and Mr. Mack, for believing in me, for helping me discover my voice, and for inspiring me to want to become an educator. Thank you.

TABLE OF CONTENTS

ACKNOWLEDGMENTS

Thank you to Kelin, Crosbie, and Scout for your unwavering love, support and encouragement.

Thank you to Mom and Dad for all of the sacrifices you have made. Thank you for pushing me to get an education. Thank you for always believing in me. Thank you for your love.

Thank you to Marty for being a kindred spirit and friend.

Thank you to these awesome and inspiring colleagues who encouraged me to write a book: Karen Freberg, Carolyn Mae Kim, Keith Quesenberry, and Ai Addyson-Zhang. I am humbled by your support.

Thank you to Anastacia Baird for inspiring me with materials to help my students create better social media content and for allowing me to adapt materials from your social media content grading rubric and your social media guidelines handout.

Thank you to the social media professors community group for your willingness to share and support all of us who are working to educate the professional communicators of tomorrow.

Thank you to the many people who helped craft the book title via MattKushin.com.

Thank you to Masahiro Yamamoto and Francis Dalisay for being such great colleagues and friends. Thank you for your editing assistance. Go Cougs!

Thank you to the Shepherd University Foundation for the financial support.

Thank you to all of the readers of my blog for your support.

And, thank you to coffee, friends, and good music.

Without any of the above, this book would not exist.

Matthew J. Kushin, Ph.D.

INTRODUCTION

This is not a textbook and it is not a workbook. It is a 'how to' book for educators about the process of teaching a social media class. It contains assignments, and activities, but it is much more than that. It is an entire plan for how you can teach a social media class.

I wrote this book because I believe that all of us who are educators in the social media space are on a common mission to bridge the gap between the classroom and the field today. I hope this book allows me play a little part in that. I have written about some of the content in this book on my social media teaching blog, MattKushin.com. But most of the content in this book is content that I have not yet shared. Further, I've never publicly organized my assignments and activities together in a systematic way that explains how to plan and execute an entire class.

There are two ways to use this book:

1. **Follow the book as an end-to-end guide for teaching your class.** You will find that this book is designed around a social media project that spans the entire semester. All of the topics, assignments and activities in this book are integrated into a social media project and therefore each chapter (and each assignment) builds upon the chapter before it. If you follow this approach, you will want to read the entire book before starting to plan your class.
2. **Picking and choosing assignments and activities to integrate into your existing class.** Call this the à la carte approach. You don't need to build your class around the semester project to apply the information in this book. Pick what works for you.

You'll note that I have not provided any lecture slides in this book or in the additional resources. My goal with this book is to coach you with a game plan. But you have to play the game. A cut-and-paste formula telling you exactly what to say would strip your class of your unique perspective, experience, and enthusiasm. Those are the things that make a class successful and make teaching enjoyable. My mission was not to write a book that made carbon copy professors and classrooms. My mission was to empower professors by showing them a path.

I started my blog, MattKushin.com, about teaching social media in 2013. I didn't expect much. I just wanted to think out loud about what I was trying to do in the classroom. I wanted to feel like I was doing my part in the conversation. I thought, maybe a few people would read the blog now and again. I thought that if something I posted helped someone else, well, that would be pretty cool. Since that time, I have published over 170 blog posts and have had tens of thousands of visits. I've met amazing people and gotten to work with them on exciting projects. Opportunities that I never could have dreamed of have been presented to me, just because I talk about what I teach – both the things that go well and the many mishaps along the way. How crazy is that?

I attribute my success to the professors and professionals I have met through social media. They are giving, caring, passionate people. I am humbled, blessed, and thankful to have such wonderful people advocate for me. Most importantly, I am inspired by their dedication to our collective work in this field.

I am proud to be part of a community of educators who are passionate about teaching and helping students. I tell you this because I hope that you share what you are doing in the classroom with our community. It makes us all a little better.

I am so thankful to you for reading this book and, most importantly, for being a colleague. I hope you enjoy it. I would love your feedback and thoughts. What would you like to see on my blog? What would you like to see in another book or in a podcast or other project? How can I get better? You can find me on Twitter @mjkushin, on Linkedin @mattkushin, on Instagram @mjkushin, in the Social Media Professors Community Group on Facebook, and of course at MattKushin.com.

If you enjoy this book, please take a few minutes to review it on Amazon. I would love it if you shared a photo of your copy of the book on social media and tagged me: @mjkushin, on Twitter, @mattkushin on Linkedin, and @mjkushin on Instagram.

I truly appreciate you.

- Matt

Additional Resources
All the assignments in the chapter appendixes and in Chapter 9 of this book are available to download. Download the zip file via the URL provided at the back of this book.
Sign up for the Social Media Syllabus blog mailing list. Go to MattKushin.com. Enter your email address and click subscribe.

CHAPTER 1: A FRAMEWORK FOR TEACHING KNOWLEDGE, SKILLS, AND ABILITIES

How do we find ways to help students learn knowledge, skills, and abilities? This chapter discusses the need to teach beyond knowledge alone and offers a simple framework for doing so.

Teaching a social media class is challenging. The field is constantly changing – what was popular a few years ago is passé today. Just ask the disenchanted devotees to services like Vine, Meerkat and many others. The good news is that apps, blogs, livestreams, short form video, long form video, and whatever is just around the corner are all merely tactics. That is, they are tools for communicating. But strategic thinking and knowing the principles of effective communication have a much longer shelf life than an app or a trend.

While the tools discussed in this book may come and go, my hope is that what you learn and apply from this book lasts longer than your best Snapstreak. That is because this book is aimed at teaching you the skills for executing a social media class using a structured approach. That approach aims to teach students adaptable knowledge and skills as well as lifelong abilities such as critical thinking, problem solving, creative thinking, and ethical decision-making.

In short, I hope this book helps you #TeachConfident when it comes to teaching social media in today's hyper-evolving digital landscape.

If we want our students to succeed as professional communicators today, we must move beyond teaching knowledge and tactics – for example, how to use social media apps - alone. We live in an environment where we need to teach knowledge, abilities, and skills. In the many conversations I have had with industry experts, I often hear the same refrain: Students today are not prepared for what the industry expects of them as entry-level employees. A disconnect exists between what students are learning in public relations, advertising, and marketing programs and what the industry is doing.

This is further evidenced by the 2017 report of undergraduate public relations education that was published by the Commission on Public Relations Education (O'Neil, Moreno, Rawlins & Valentini, 2018). The report states that practitioners seek entry-level employees with skills in social media management, research and analytics, writing, communication and editing. Yet, those practitioners reported that entry-level employees do not have these skills at the levels they are desired. The same is true for abilities. Practitioners want, but are not getting to the extent desired, entry-level employees with the following abilities: Creative thinking, problem solving, critical thinking, analytical thinking, and strategic planning.

I think this is what students want too. My evidence is only anecdotal but I often hear students talk about the magic word "application." They will say something like, "in your classes I learn a lot because we're always applying what we learn." In fact, I was talking to a student this morning who told me: "Your classes are tough, because we have to apply it." She wasn't talking about a social media or technology-heavy class. She was talking about a persuasion theory class I teach where the projects require students to apply what they learned to design campaign messages.

So, how do we address the gap between what practitioners want and what students are learning?

There are many amazing professors working on just this very problem. At the end of this chapter, I will provide a list of professors, groups, and blogs I strongly encourage you to check out. In this book, I'm going to share how I am seeking to address this gap. It is based on a simple, easy-to-apply framework for teaching. But first, here are my goals for this book:

1. **To provide you an end-to-end plan for teaching a social media class at the university level (or elsewhere).** Want a syllabus that you can use? Love sample assignments? Lecture ideas? Activities for applying concepts? Boom. Boom. Boom. Boom! I've got them in this book.

2. **To help you execute this plan with minimal funding and few external resources.** Let's face it, funding is tight at universities today. If you work at a regional or small university like I do, chances are that there is little funding for you to buy software or expensive equipment. If you work in a rural region away from industry like I do, it can be very hard to find a class client. This book will give you everything you need to effectively teach a social media class where your students get hands-on experience creating and executing a social media plan without costly software and without the need for an external class client; although you are welcome to use one if you like (We'll talk about that decision later).

3. **To help you turn your class into a quasi-agency.** Let me say it again. Your students will create and execute a social media plan for a real organization with real followers. It will be like your class is its own quasi-agency. The plan I lay out in this book is aimed at teaching your students the necessary skills, abilities and knowledge to do so.

4. **To help you apply the What, Why, How, Do, Reflect (WWHDR) framework in your teaching approach.** What the heck is that? Don't worry, you don't have to love acronyms to succeed at this. After all, there are no tests in this class. I'll explain below.

5. **To help you take more risks while maintaining professional control of your class and its direction.** Risk taking is something I have struggled with as

a professor. I'm a bit of a control freak. I hate not knowing what's happening on any given day in my class. In life and in teaching, I love predictability. But, in a media landscape that is constantly experimenting with new tools – from live video to virtual reality - educators must cultivate a mindset of experimentation too. So, the approach I take in this book will seek to balance risk-taking (via the work your students do for the class client) while also existing in a very Matt Kushin kind of world: A world where we know where we're going and why.

The What, Why, How, Do, Reflect (WWHDR) Framework

I'll admit it. I have tried but I have not thought of a cooler, more memorable acronym for the framework I'm about to explain. I know WWHDR is a bit clunky. But what it lacks in creative naming I hope it makes up for in application.

This book will use the WWHDR framework for organizing at the micro level (that is, lessons) and at the macro level (that is, units).

The good news is that I'm not teaching you something that you don't already know. I'm just putting it in a system that will make lesson planning more efficient. Chances are, you're already doing several of these steps, but you may not have strung them all together in a systematic fashion. Codifying the process will help you be mindful of how you are organizing lessons and units, and thus your entire class. The more mindful you are of what you're doing, the more purpose-driven your classes will be. You'll feel more prepared and you'll be able to articulate to your students WHY they are learning the class subject matter. This WHY is a key ingredient for a rewarding learning environment.

When it all comes together, you just may allow yourself to feel more relaxed because you'll be walking into the classroom saying to yourself, "I got this!" #TeachConfident.

Sounds like a lot from a little system, right? But these are the outcomes that I've gotten from codifying this approach to teaching. I hope you gain some of these benefits too.

Learning Goals

If you don't know what you want students to learn, how can you teach it to them?

Start by identifying what you want your students to learn from the lesson or unit you are planning. These are your learning goals, aka learning objectives. With the WWHDR framework, you're going to be teaching knowledge, abilities and skills. So you may want a learning goal for each.

Here's an example:

1. **Knowledge Learning Goal(s):** I want my students to know what sentiment

analysis of social media posts is and how it works.

2. **Abilities Learning Goal(s):** I want my students to develop their critical thinking and analytical thinking abilities when it comes to interpreting sentiment analysis results. It is important that they question how the sentiment score is calculated.

3. **Skills Learning Goal(s):** I want my students to be able to dive into the data to question the results of the sentiment analysis by qualitatively assessing a sample of the social media posts used to develop the sentiment score.

Notice how all three are related. But in particular, notice how the abilities are necessary to the understanding of the limitations of sentiment analysis. In this instance, I want my students to know not to take a sentiment score at face value because machine coding of social posts is limited in its accuracy (Dalisay, Kushin & Yamamoto, 2017). Therefore, students need to analyze and think critically about the sentiment score they find. This blends into the skills learning. Students need to both be able to interpret the score on its surface as well as be able to assess the actual data to see if the software appears to be scoring social media posts inaccurately. Taken together, the students are learning to take the score as a quick 'rule of thumb' that requires a deeper dive.

Once we have our learning goals, we start building our lesson, thus beginning the What, Why, How, Do and Reflect portions of the framework.

1. **What:** What is the topic you are teaching? Execute your knowledge learning goal(s) here. You can deliver the knowledge through a brief lecture or presentation. Include background information, key terms, examples and case studies, and other important information necessary for understanding the subject matter.

2. **Why:** Why is the learner learning this? Often, students ask this very question. So preempt them by explicating the connection between the subject matter and its purpose. This can be done as part of the brief lecture or you can help students convince themselves of the Why by posing the question to the class and allowing the students to offer answers. This can help students think through why this knowledge is important and may help the Why stick. A personally meaningful learning experience can be a powerful one. So don't forget the Why section. There are many creative ways to show the Why. For example, you can show the why by pointing out the consequences, both positive and negative, of knowing or not knowing the knowledge you are teaching or from doing or not doing a particular action related to the skills or abilities you are teaching.

3. **How:** How will the learner apply the knowledge? In this stage, show students the How through such means as in-class guidance, text or multimedia tutorials, and brief lectures or conversations emphasizing

need-to-know information and important considerations the learner needs to effectively execute the task. Everyone learns differently and at different paces. By offering multiple modalities and resources for learning, you can empower students to learn in a way that works best for them. Some students learn by seeing examples, others prefer to read through instructions, and others want hands-on help. Just keep in mind that the How section is where we often hit a pitfall when we teach something. We ask the learner to do something without providing adequate instruction and guidance.

4. **Do:** What do you want your students to be able to do? This is activity time and it goes hand-in-hand with the How stage. So, the two may be running concurrently. Execute your skills learning goal(s) as well as your abilities learning goal(s). The more practice the student gets, the better. Students will have questions and will struggle here. It shows that they are learning. When I first started teaching, I was quick to solve their problems. But I've changed my approach over the years. I ask myself, what would Socrates do? Now, I ask guiding questions and help the students learn to think through the problems.

5. **Reflect:** What knowledge, skills, and abilities do you want to reinforce? This is an important but often-skipped stage in the framework. By asking the student to reflect on what they learned, why they did it, how they did it, and what they did, connections can be made, learning strengthened, and abilities developed. Use tools such as class discussion, learner-to-learner discussion, and written or verbal feedback.

It is easy to apply this framework in building a lesson or unit plan. Open your word processor and create a template. At the top, write knowledge learning goal(s), abilities learning goal(s) and skills learning goal(s). Below, write What, Why, How, Do, Reflect. Save the template and use it each time you are building a lesson.

Further, I've applied this framework to classes where technology plays little part. I teach a persuasion and message design course that is built around discussing theories and strategies of persuasion. While that class spends more time on the What and the Why stages, I use the How Do and Reflect as well through group projects and in-class activities. For example, I have a "persuasion in action" section where I show students how to apply the theories and strategies from class to their day-to-day lives. I ask them to reflect on times when they've experienced these theories and strategies in their lives to enhance critical thinking and ethical decision making skills.

In the chapters ahead, I will use the WWHDR framework to lay out the lessons and by extension, the units. I will refer to each part of the framework so you can clearly see how it is being applied.

Requirements

This book presents a hands-on, engaged learning environment. As I will mention repeatedly in this book, I am a proponent of having your students work on projects in class. Because this class is focused on technology, your class will be most successful if students have access to computers. If possible, teach this class in a computer lab classroom. If that is not possible, see if there is a computer lab on campus, such as in the library, that your class can use occasionally. Schedule your class in the computer lab on the lab days listed in the syllabus (see the Chapter 2 appendix). Alternatively, you may require your students to bring laptops to class. All of the software needed in this class can be accessed via the web. Laptops are expensive and not all students can afford them. If you are requiring students to bring their own laptops, you may want to ensure that each student group has one or two members who own a laptop. So long as each student group has access to one or two computers, they will be able to do the work.

Recommended Social Media Resources: Professors, Groups and Lists

Below is a list of professors doing amazing things in and around the social media education space. These are brilliant, innovative people dedicated to preparing students to succeed in a world of change. I have been fortunate to chat with them, work with them on projects, and see what their students are accomplishing. They inspire me every day.

Twitter

Josie Ahlquist • @josieahlquist
Lucinda Austin • @LucindaLAustin
Anastacia Baird • @ProfBaird
Kelli S. Burns • @KelliSBurns
Scott Cowley • @scottcowley
Karen Freberg • @kfreberg
Tiffany Gallicano • @Gallicano
Amber Hutchins • @amberhutchins
Melissa Janoske McLean • @mjresearch
Carolyn Mae Kim • @CarolynMaeKim
Emily Kinsky • @ekinsky
Jeremy H. Lipschultz • @JeremyHL
Chuck Lubbers • @DRChuckLubbers
Kelli Mathews • @kmathews
Stefanie Moore • @StefMoore
Leo Morejon • @MoreLeo

Emi Moriuchi • @e_moriuchi
Holly Overton • @hkoverton
Katie R. Place • @KatiePlace
Geah Pressgrove • @GeahPressgrove
Keith A. Quesenberry • @Kquesen
Cindy Royal • @CindyRoyal
Gary Schirr • @ProfessorGary
Diana Sisson • @saysdiana
Don Stanley • @3rhinomedia
Kathleen Stansberry • @kstansberry
Karen E. Sutherland • @kesutherland777
Adrienne Wallace • @adriwall
Amanda J. Weed • @amandajweed
Ai Addyson-Zhang • @aiaddysonzhang

Blogs

Don Stanley • http://www.432.3rhinoacademy.com/
Gary Schirr • https://smm4biz.com/
Karen Freberg • https://karenfreberg.com/blog/blog/
Karen Sutherland • https://drkarensutherland.com/blog/
Ai Addyson-Zhang • https://medium.com/@aiaddysonzhang

A few other sources you may find helpful are below:

The Social Media Professors Twitter account:
https://twitter.com/SMprofessors
The Social Media Professors Facebook group:
https://www.facebook.com/groups/socialmediaprofessors/
A Twitter list of outstanding social media academics I cultivate:
https://twitter.com/mjkushin/lists/academia/members
A Twitter list of strategic communication accounts I cultivate:
https://twitter.com/mjkushin/lists/strategic

Matthew J. Kushin, Ph.D.

CHAPTER 2: THE SOCIAL MEDIA PROJECT THAT GUIDES THIS CLASS

What is the social media project and how does it relate to the quasi-agency model? What are the assignments that make up the project? What do I need to prepare ahead of time? This chapter explains the project, how it works, and shows you how to apply it in your classes.

The social media project is the centerpiece of the class that you will teach with the guidance of this book. In this chapter, I will introduce you to the project and cover important considerations.

About the Project

The social media project is the research, planning, execution, monitoring and – to an extent – evaluation of a social media campaign. In other words, your students are going to run the social media for a class client.

It is going to be a ton of fun. Your class will be filled with creative energy. Your students will create content they can be proud of. When interviewing for a job, your students will be able to explain the strategy behind the content they created. Yes, they can use this content in their portfolio when searching for jobs.

There are several assignments over the course of the semester which comprise the semester-long project. These assignments build upon one another. The class is broken down into six units. Below each unit I have listed the assignments related to the semester-long class project:

1. Onboarding Students
    - *Assignment:* None.
2. Social Media Listening
    - *Assignment:* Social Media Audit
3. The Strategic Brief
    - *Assignment:* The Strategic Brief & Presentation
4. Content 1, Social Media Influencers and Content Creation Best Practices
    - *Assignment:* Content #1 & Presentation
5. Content 2, Social Media Metrics, and Ongoing Social Listening
    - *Assignment:* Content #2 & Presentation
6. Content 3 and Paid Social Media Advertising
    - *Assignment:* Content #3 & Presentation

The Quasi-Agency Model

Your class will follow a quasi-agency model, meaning that you will act as if your class is an agency taking on a client. As the professor, you are the account supervisor and your students make up your team on the account. You will be teaching your students not only how professional and strategic social media is done, but enabling them to learn by actually doing it. The students will also learn the basics of the strategic campaign planning process, which you or other faculty in your department can build upon in a campaigns class.

Tell your students the above information and tell them that you expect them to behave as if they are working for a client. Tell them that this class is about hands-on learning and that you have high expectations of their work. Tell them that only outstanding content will be published.

Choosing a Class Client

Client-class fit is important. You as the professor have to manage the expectations of your client and your students. I work with external clients in other classes and it has been great. It is a very rewarding experience. Students learn a ton and build their portfolio. But for my social media class, I take a different approach.

The level of control that you have as the professor in this class is very important. While it might be exciting to work with an outside organization, perhaps even a well-known brand or non-profit, it is likely that those organizations are going to want strict control over everything that gets published on their social media. While there are many upsides to this, it is going to make your job a lot harder. If the client is constantly putting up roadblocks, the students will never publish anything, and their learning will suffer because they won't be able to see the fruits of their labor or monitor their success (As you'll see in chapters 7 and 8 in the Content Period 2 and Content Period 3 units of the semester, students will learn to monitor the engagement of the social media they create).

We'll be doing a lot in this class and roadblocks can put you behind. Therefore, I recommend choosing a client that gives you a degree of freedom over what gets published. The solution that has worked for me is to run the social media for my department at Shepherd University, the department of communication. This set up is not uncommon[1]. Benefits include:

1.   My department and I have established an understanding of what type of

---

[1] A poll of the Social Media Professors Facebook group by Professor Anastacia Baird on October 18, 2018 found that 10 professors reported managing their department's social media presence through a class.
See:
https://facebook.com/groups/1764961653763282?view=permalink&id=2155497
588043018

content we are looking for.

2. Because I've worked with the department as my client for several years, I don't have to onboard them each time. Expectations are clear on both sides.
3. I have a lot of editorial control over the type of content that we publish.
4. I have password access to all of the social media accounts for our department and can share it with students when needed.
5. I am responsible for what gets posted.
6. Because my university is located in a rural area, we don't have a lot of access to potential clients. Using our department as a client helps me overcome this issue.
7. Because there is no external client involved, managing everything is much simpler.
8. Because the students are all familiar with the department and university, little time is wasted getting them up to speed on the client.

Wouldn't it be better to work with an organization outside of your department? In a lot of ways, yes. But keep in mind that you are going to teach your students all of the same knowledge, abilities and skills that you would be teaching them if you were to work with an external client.

So consider the level of control that the class client is going to give you. If you are comfortable working with an outside organization, large or small, that's great. Be sure to have a conversation with the organization to explain what your goals are. If you choose to use an on-campus organization or, like me, your department as a client, have those same conversations with your client. In working with your client, make sure that expectations are set from the get go and clear communication is established. Here are a few questions to ask:

1. Who is your target audience?
2. What are your social media goals?
3. What does success in this project look like to you?
4. Do you have social media guidelines or policies that I can share with my students?
5. Do you have an existing social media strategy? If so, do you expect us to follow it or are we allowed to develop something new?
6. What type of content is your organization looking for when it comes to social media?
7. What type of content do you not want us to create? Is there any type of content that should be avoided or that is prohibited?
8. What does the approval process look like for getting the content that our students will be creating published on your social media channels?
9. How long does that approval process take?
10. What are your expectations for the content that our students will be producing?

11. What concerns do you have in working with students on this project?
12. What other things do I need to make sure my students are aware of when it comes to creating content for your organization?

Setting Up the "Background Information" For this Project

Once you have solidified a class client, you will need some basic background information that will be used to help onboard your students to the project. Because this class is about teaching students to strategically plan and create content, we are going to ground what they do in the context of a strategic plan. The students in your class will use this background information and build off of its foundation, launching them directly into the planning stage of the project.

If you are familiar with strategic campaign planning, then you are familiar with the four (or three, depending how you teach it) stages of the campaign process[2]. They are: 1) Defining the problem or opportunity, 2) planning and programming, 3) taking action and communication, and 4) evaluating the program (Broom & Shaw, 2013).

For this project, we are going to create some of the necessary background research that would be completed in the 1) defining the problem or opportunity and 2) planning and programming stages.

If you are working with a client, then get the necessary information directly from them. If you are working with your department, then work with your department to build this information. Here's what you need:

1. **Goals:** What are the client's goals for this social media campaign?

Example: To increase awareness of the XYZ University communication department throughout campus, in the community, and among our prospective students.

2. **Objectives:** What are the client's Specific Measurable Achievable Relevant and Time Bound (S.M.A.R.T.) objectives for this social media campaign? You can draft these or have your students create their own. I prefer to provide one objective and allow the students to create a secondary objective.

Example: To increase the number of current students who follow our social

---

[2] While there are several different configurations for the campaign planning process, with some configurations containing three stages as in the third edition of Randy Bobbitt and Ruth Sullivan's *Developing the Public Relations Campaign: A Team-Based Approach*, this book will apply the four-stage planning process as adapted from *Cutlip & Center's Effective Public Relations* by Gen M. Broom and Bey-Ling Sha. It's not vital that you follow one approach or the other so long as your students understand the approach you are using.

media accounts by 25% over the course of the semester.

3. **Audiences:** What are your primary and secondary audiences?[3]

Example:
Primary audiences: 1) current students who major or minor in communication; 2) potential major and minor students (transfers from other departments, transfers from other schools, or incoming freshmen).
Secondary audiences: 1) Parents of current or potential students; 2) The wider university community; 3) The wider community in our region.

4. **Campaign Theme:** The theme guides the focus of your campaign. It is an overarching idea that applies to all your audiences. It could be a slogan, a creative concept, an event, a holiday, or other tie in around which the campaign is organized.

Example: The communication department is the university's "best kept secret." Note that this theme ties into the weakness in our S.W.O.T. analysis below.

5. **Key Messages:** Your key messages are the ideas that encircle your communication efforts – they permeate the content your students will create.

Example: Our department is a place to grow creatively; Our department classes are exciting, dynamic, relevant and innovative; Our graduates are savvy with technology, professional and self-motivated.

6. **Social Media Channel Purpose Statement:** This statement helps ground each social media channel. It is a quick sentence or two describing what the purpose of that social media channel will be. It will help your students focus their efforts. You can draft this or have your students create their own. I prefer to provide examples and then let students modify them.

Example: Twitter - A way to share brief information, news, updates, and reminders about events and important deadlines. The tone is welcoming and fun.

7. **S.W.O.T. Analysis:** – What are the internal strengths and weaknesses of your client? What are the external opportunities and threats? You'll want several for each category. In the example below, I will provide one for

---

[3] Primary audiences are the principal, intended target of your communication. They are in a decision-making position. Secondary audiences are groups that would also benefit from your message.

each category.

Example:
Strength – The technology equipment available to our students, including two computer labs with industry-leading software, a state-of-the-art television studio and our radio station.
Weakness – The location of our department is in part of the building that most people never travel to so students don't know everything we have to offer.
Opportunity – The location of our university to several small and large cities;
Threats – There are many other universities within a few hours' drive.

That's all the background information you need to get your students started. Depending on time and availability, you can add other background information as well, such as a mission statement, a vision statement, information about the organization, and so forth. By providing your students with the background information, you will increase consistency in focus across your student teams. Below, I discuss how your students will work together in teams to run a social media channel for your client.

Dividing Your Class Into Teams

Your students will work in teams, with each team taking on a different social media channel. The number of teams will depend on the number of students you have and the number of social media channels your class will be managing.

In my class, there are usually four teams with about four or five students in each team. The social media channels are: Twitter, Instagram and Snapchat. One team also runs the department blog[4].

Feel free to get creative and remember that it's your class, so make it what you want. We've considered creating a podcast and using that as a channel.

If your university department is your client and you don't have a social media channel, this will be your chance to create it. I started our Instagram and Snapchat accounts, our Twitter account existed when I was hired. A few years ago, I avoided using Snapchat because metrics are hard to follow. But, I capitulated because of its popularity and because my classes were large enough that I needed a fourth social media channel. As you'll see in later assignments, the team that picks Snapchat has to do a lot of extra work to stay on top of it when collecting metrics. Therefore, I suggest avoiding Snapchat if you can.

---

[4] Many organizations do not consider blogs as part of their social media mix. Blogs are often used for SEO and other business purposes, such as sales. In this book, blogs will be discussed alongside social media because blogs are a great platform for learning to create and promote content.

If your class is very large or you do not have many social media channels to manage, then adjustments may be necessary. Try having multiple teams work on the same social media channel. For example, you may have two teams handling Instagram. One team is in charge of a certain type of content on Instagram – say, creating content for Instagram stories – and the other team is in charge of a different type of content – say, feed posts. Another option is to have a team that is responsible for IGTV content. My class will be experimenting with IGTV in Fall 2019.

In the next chapter, I will provide tips on forming teams and provide several checks and balances that I use to make sure teams work effectively.

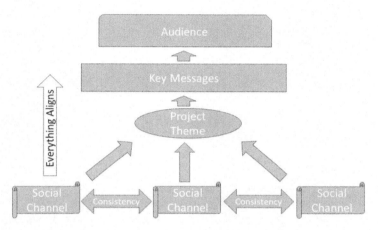

Image 1. A conceptual framework for organizing the "Background Information" for this project and its relation to the social channels your students will be creating content for.

Questions, Comments, Concerns - Oh, My!

I hope you are getting excited about implementing this into your class. But, I bet you have some questions and concerns.

Certainly, there are a number of risks involved in putting your students in charge of running social media for an organization. What if the students create poor quality content? What if the content they create isn't appropriate?

There are a number of checks and balances you can implement to curb these risks. For example, as you will see in Chapter 5, students will create a strategic brief that articulates their group's overall content plan for the semester. Also, you will give students feedback that will steer their plan and help them stay on track. You can do this through written feedback, group meetings, or whatever method you feel works best.

Further, when students create content, they will not be simply creating content and posting it to social media. There is a built-in editorial process. I will describe this process in detail in Chapter 6. For now, just know that your students will plan their content ahead of time. They will present that content to the class. The other students in the class will provide verbal feedback to the group and ask questions while also completing a worksheet which they will turn into you. Because your students will be evaluating their peers and providing you with written feedback via the worksheet, the extra eyes can help bring to light things that you did not see or consider. You will thus have a chance to review and approve or deny all content before it is posted.

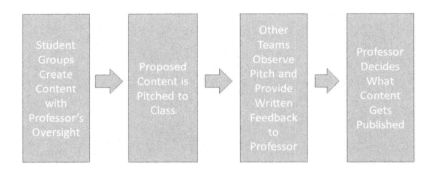

Image 2. The gatekeeper workflow for this project.

You may also have mixed feelings about having students work in teams. I understand. I was that way too. But ever since I saw a presentation by Dr. Larry Michaelsen on team-based learning while I was on faculty at Utah Valley University, I have been a fan of team-based projects in my classes. Every one of my classes now requires students to work in teams in some capacity. There are, of course, benefits and drawbacks to this. Common drawbacks include unequal workloads, interpersonal conflict, poor communication, leadership vacuums, and groupthink, among others. I have dealt with all of these drawbacks and I know I will continue to. In Chapter 3, I will provide a number of resources for helping manage teams, or I should say, helping teams manage themselves. Despite the drawbacks, here are some benefits to team-based learning:

1. **Peer-based learning:** Students don't just learn from you. They learn from one another. Peer-based learning has received scholarly attention in psychology and education circles. A student's classmates have unique perspectives, knowledge, skills and abilities that the student doesn't have. By engaging in tasks such as discussing ideas, working through problems collaboratively, and explaining what they are learning to fellow

students, students are actively engaged in learning[5].

2. **Skills Learning:** Students can develop important skills and abilities. These include teamwork, interpersonal skills, effective communication, leadership, group decision-making, critical thinking, problem solving, among others.

3. **Classroom Management:** A classroom is much more manageable when you are providing help to a few groups as opposed to 20 individuals. Consider how much more time you will have to provide in-class support to teams as well as to manage team meetings during office hours.

4. **Less grading:** The math is simple. Imagine that in Class A you have 20 students and each student does a project. In Class B you have 20 students divided in teams of four, such that there are 5 groups. Each group does a project. In Class B your grading load is 25% that of your grading load in Class A.

Sample Syllabus

A sample syllabus for a class that meets twice a week is available in the chapter appendix.

Recommended Readings and More

Readings

Clayton, B. & Ordway, D.M. (n.d.). How social media may influence student loyalty to a university. *Harvard Kennedy School Shorenstein Center on Media, Politics and Public Policy Journalist's Resource*. Retrieved from https://journalistsresource.org/studies/society/education/social-media-university-student-brand-loyalty/

Websites

https://teambasedlearning.org.

---

[5] To learn more about what peer-based learning is, see Damon, W. (1984). Peer education: The untapped potential. *Journal of Applied Developmental Psychology, 5*(4), 331-343. If you prefer a quick primer on peer-based learning and its benefits, I recommend this essay by David Boud, published on Stanford's "Tomorrow's Professor Postings" blog. https://tomprof.stanford.edu/posting/418. You may also enjoy this brief summary of peer-based learning written by Matthew C.E. Gwee, which can be found at http://www.cdtl.nus.edu.sg/success/sl13.htm

Chapter 2 Appendix

Sample Syllabus for Course That Meets Twice a Week During the Fall Semester Over a Period of 15 Weeks

Class: Strategic Social Media
3 Credit Hours

Location:
Time:

Text:

Professor:
Email:
Phone
Office:
Office Hours:

Course Description

The course explores the role of social media in public relations, marketing and related fields. It helps students develop knowledge, skills, and abilities relevant to careers in strategic communication. Students will investigate professional, theoretical, cultural, and societal aspects of social media and will gain a better understanding of its impact on the relationships between society, organizations, and commerce.

Assessment based on ability to:

- Complete a semester-long project involving planning, executing, and evaluating social media for a class client.
- Give professional group presentations.
- Meet deadlines.
- Work effectively in teams to solve problems and complete projects.
- Utilize technology to improve writing and visual communication.
- Develop the key abilities of: Critical thinking, creative thinking, problem solving, and analytical abilities.
- Demonstrate the application of these abilities as they relate to the strategic use of new and social communication technologies for businesses and organizations and individual career advancement.
- Demonstrate the application of these abilities as they relate to paid social media.
- Apply these abilities to the strategic applications of social media measurement tools, with a focus on four intertwined areas:
  - *Monitoring:* Strategies for identifying, cultivating, monitoring, and analyzing information on the social web.
  - *Metrics:* Strategies for setting goals and what to measure on social media.
  - *Optimization:* Strategic use of optimization strategies to

maximize potential exposure to and engagement with communication content online.

o *Content & Engagement:* Strategies for creating content targeted towards online audiences and encouraging their engagement with organization.

Major Assignments

- Participation and Activities
- Facebook Advertising Case Study Presentation Assignment
- Social Media Case Study Paper
- Team Evaluations (2)
- Social Media Project which is made up of the following:
  o Social Media Audit Assignment
  o Strategic Brief Assignment
  o Content Period 1 and Presentation
  o Content Period 2 and Presentation
  o Content Period 3 and Presentation

Week & Day	Topic	Assignments A = assign D = due H = Homework I = In-class activity
Week 1 Day 1	Welcome to Class and Introduction of Social Media Semester Project	
Day 2	Background Plan Overview; Team Formation	I: Form Teams I: Team Contracts H: *Generation Like* documentary
Week 2 Day 3	An Overview of Social Media Listening	I: Keywords Activity I: Social Media Listening Activity
Day 4	Social Listening Activities Lab Day	I: The Audience Analysis Activity
Week 3 Day 5	The Social Media Audit	A: The Social Media Audit Assignment
Day 6	Social Media Audit Lab Day	
Week 4 Day 7	Why People Share Content; Content Categories	D: The Social Media Audit Assignment
Day 8	Brainstorm Content Categories; Introduce Content Calendars; Content Calendars Brainstorm	
Week 5 Day 9	Strategic Brief Assignment; Lab Day to Work on Strategic Brief	A: Strategic Brief Assignment

		Assignment
Day 10	Half of Class is a Lab Day and Half of Class Students Present Strategic Briefs	I: Team Evaluation 1 D: Strategic Brief Assignment
Week 6 Day 11	Assignment Overview and Introduction to Influencers	A: Content Period 1 I: Evaluating Influencers Activity
Day 12	Digital Influencers and Lab Time to Work on Content Period 1 and Finding Influencers	I: Influencer/ Brand Fit Activity
Week 7 Day 13	Content Period 1 Lab Day (Optional: Social Media Content Creation Best Practices)	
Day 14	Student Presentations	D: Content Period 1 and Presentations
Week 8 Day 15	Assignment Overview and Introducing Social Media Metrics	A: Content Period 2
Day 16	Social Media Metrics: Planning and Metrics Goals Lecture and Metrics Lab Time	
Week 9 Day 17	Content Optimization Lecture and Optimization Lab Time Note: Begin weekly metrics tracking	
Day 18	Social Media Listening and Listening Lab Time	
Week 10 Day 19	Content Period 2 Lab Day	
Day 20	Student Presentations	D: Content Period 2 and Presentations
Week 11 Day 21	What is Paid Social Media Advertising and How Does it Work?; Introduce Facebook Advertising Case Study Assignment (optional)	A: Content Period 3 A: Facebook Advertising Case Study Presentation Assignment (optional)
Day 22	Facebook Advertising Case Study Presentation Assignment Lab Time (optional)	
Week 12 Day 23	Objective-oriented, Targeting Advertising Campaigns	I: Create a Campaign and Ad Set in the Facebook Ads Manager Activity D: First half of

		presentations - Facebook Advertising Case Study Presentation Assignment (optional)
Day 24	Ad Creative	I: Create a Social Media Advertisement in the Facebook Creative Hub Activity D: Second half of presentations - Facebook Advertising Case Study Presentation Assignment (optional)
Week 13 Day 25	Thanksgiving Break	
Day 26	Thanksgiving Break	
Week 14 Day 27	Introduce Campaign Reporting and the Use of Data to Improve Advertising Success; Facebook Campaign Reporting and Data Knowledge Check Activity	
Day 28	Catch up time as needed; Content 3 work day	I: Facebook Campaign Reporting and Data Knowledge Check Activity
Week 15 Day 29	Content 3 work day	
Day 30	Content 3 presentations	I: Team Evaluation 2 D: Content Period 3 and Presentations

Course Policies

Participation Grade: A portion of your grade comes from participation. This grade is calculated based on activities I will assign throughout the semester, general participation in classroom discussion and evidence of preparation (e.g., attending class having completed the readings), as well as the student's contribution to a productive, inclusive and respectful educational environment for the professor and fellow students.

Attendance, Being On Time, and Leaving Early:
Class participation is important for the success of the class and to your success. You are expected to attend class regularly and on time and to stay for the duration of class.

Classroom Environment: Play (smartphones, games on handheld devices, etc.), reading non-course related materials, or working on assignments for other classes is distracting. We're all here to learn and people pay a lot of money for their education. Use of Internet devices to take notes and gather information to inform classroom discussion is strongly encouraged. But browsing and social interaction are not so please minimize use during class. If your use of any device becomes disruptive, it will negatively impact your participation grade. If your ringer goes off during class, please turn it off. If you feel the call may be an emergency, please step out of class.

Late assignments: Late means turned in ANYTIME AFTER the end of scheduled class time on the due date. Two minutes late and 2 hours late are treated equally. Late assignments will be accepted for a 20% reduction in grade. Late assignments will not be accepted beyond one class period late. Students are responsible for remembering to turn in assignments (online for major papers) or in person prior to end of class on the due date. In the rare case that a student is not able to attend class on the date an assignment is due, the student may submit the assignment electronically BEFORE the end of class on the assigned day for full credit. There will be no exceptions to the late assignment policy.

CHAPTER 3: UNIT 1. ONBOARDING STUDENTS

The first unit of the semester acquaints students with the class and the semester social media project. It also serves to assist students in forming their teams for the project.

We start the semester by onboarding your class to the social media project. The suggested schedules throughout this book are based on a course that meets twice a week with each class lasting one hour and fifteen minutes. Please modify the schedule to fit your needs.

Suggested Schedule: Week 1

1. Day 1: Welcome to Class and Introduction of Social Media Semester Project
2. Day 2: Background Plan Overview; Team Formation

Unit Learning Objectives

1. Onboard the students to the semester social media project.
2. Introduce students to the following concepts: 1) The PESO (paid, earned, shared, and owned media) model, 2) content marketing, 2) and narrowcasting.
3. Guide students through the team-forming process with the goal of increasing the likelihood that teams will work together effectively.

The What, Why, How, Do, Reflect

In each chapter I will break down each learning objective above into its appropriate stages within the What, Why, How, Do, Reflect (WWHDR) framework.

Learning Objective 1: Semester Social Media Project

What

Students need to know what the semester project is and its purpose.

Introduce the class client and explain that the class will run as a quasi-agency with you, the professor, serving as the account supervisor, and they, the students, working on the account. This can be done through lecture slides. Share with them the different social media platforms that they will be in charge of and explain how teams will be divided up such that each team will be in charge of a different social media platform.

Why

The students are doing the project to gain hands-on experience planning and executing social media for a client. Continue reading to see how you will also help the students discover the meaning of the project.

How and Do

In this activity, the How and Do go hand in hand. You are going to explain to your students how this project will help them gain experience by having them do a little activity.

For the How, your goal is to connect the semester social media project with the Why above. That is, you want to show how the skills the students will learn completing this project will help them prepare for an internship or career in the field.

Now for the 'Do.' Ask students what skills they think someone needs who plans to intern or work in social media, public relations, marketing or a related field today. Make a list on the board. Then, have students search for jobs with 'public relations' and/or 'social media' and/or 'marketing', et cetera, in the title on job sites like Indeed.com. Discuss with the class what knowledge, ability and skill requirements are common across the job postings. Make a list on the board. Then, connect back to the 'How' by explaining how the project will provide students with opportunities to develop skills on the list. For example, if students find that these jobs require social media monitoring and analytics skills, explain how they will get practice developing these skills in this project because they will be monitoring the success of the client's accounts (we will discuss social media metrics in Chapter 7). Inform the students that the work they do can go into their professional portfolio, which can be useful when applying for internships and jobs.

In so doing, break down how the project will work. While you don't need to overwhelm students by going into details of every assignment throughout the semester, it is important to emphasize the multi-assignment structure of the project (as discussed in Chapter 2).

Reflect

Ask the students to return to the job postings they had viewed. Ask them to assess their own knowledge, skills, and abilities against those the job or internship requires. Discuss as a class what knowledge, skills, and abilities the students feel they need to develop to be successful candidates for the job or internship they are interested in. Lastly, ask students to reflect upon what they hope to get out of the project. The goal here is to connect the project to the students' career goals and make them aware of how their work in this project will help them achieve those career goals.

Learning Objective 2: Introduce Students to Related Concepts

What

In Chapter 2, I explained that you will need to set up some basic background information about your client in the Setting Up the 'Background Information' For this Project section.

We will now orient your students to this information. Through a brief lecture you can provide students with this information, explaining that they will use this background information when they build their strategic brief assignments, which we will discuss in Chapter 5. I also like to give them this information condensed into a handout that I share through the course management system (CMS). This way, they can reference the information later when they work on their strategic brief assignments.

Next, what are the key, introductory concepts your students need to know to orient them to the project? There are many directions one could go with this. I try to focus in on a few things that will help ground students. Specifically, I cover the PESO (paid, earned, shared, and owned media) media model, content marketing, and narrowcasting.

I like to review the PESO model because it grounds the students in the larger media mix. I discuss how we are going to be working primarily in the shared media section of the landscape, but that we will also discuss influencer engagement which bleeds into the earned media section. We will also cover paid media when we learn about social media advertising through the Facebook Ads Manager (discussed in Chapter 8). You can find an article and a visualization of the PESO model on the Spin Sucks blog here:

- https://spinsucks.com/communication/pr-pros-must-embrace-the-peso-model/.

I also like to review the concept of content marketing to help orient students into why we are creating content on behalf of a brand. Find a definition of content marketing and examples on this post by the Content Marketing Institute:

- https://contentmarketinginstitute.com/what-is-content-marketing/.

Lastly, I explain that we are narrowcasting our content. Because there is high competition with so many organizations creating content online, we have to truly know our audience and create content that is not meant to please and appeal to all persons, but to the very specific audience that we want to reach; an audience that we know intimately (Goncalves, Kostakos & Venkatanathan, 2013)[6].

Why

In regard to the client background information, it suffices to let the students know during your brief lecture that they will be using this information in building their strategic brief assignments. This information will also be serving as a filter through which they will approach many of the other assignments and activities in the semester ahead.

Note that there is no How, Do, Reflect section for this material because there will be many How, Do, and Reflect sections built into the entire semester around this material. It could be said that the entire rest of the semester, in one way or another, will serve as how, do, and reflect opportunities with this material.

Learning Objective 3: Build Teams

It's time to start building student teams. Before we get into the What, Why, How, Do, Reflect (WWHDR) process, let's cover some background. I allow my students to form their own teams because it puts the responsibility on the students to take ownership of their group's success. There are a few tools that I use to encourage students to be stewards of their team. They are: Team contracts, team roles, team evaluations, and the right to fire team members. I will discuss these in the Drilldown: Group Checks and Balances section of this chapter.

How will students be assigned to each social media platform? Approach this in whatever way you feel is most equitable. I have each team pick their top two choices. If only one team wants a particular platform as either their first or second choice, then that team gets that platform. If there are multiple

---

[6] While only a cursory explanation of narrowcasting is needed for the purpose of this lecture, you may be interested to learn more about narrowcasting research. If so, see the citation for the 2013 study by Goncalves, Kostakos & Venkatanathan in the references at the end of this book.

teams that want a platform, then students have two options: 1) They negotiate among themselves – which happens in most cases because between the remaining groups there is often something that each team will be happy with, or 2) If students cannot work the problem out for themselves, I assign a number to each of the remaining teams (e.g., one through four) and choose a number at random from Random.org. The team whose number came up gets their top choice. I repeat this process as necessary.

For now, let's discuss the team forming activity of the unit which takes place in class.

What

Explain to your students that this class is going to require a lot of group work and that they should be discerning in building their teams. In this class, students will form their teams. But before they do, they are going to get a chance to hear from each student in the class, with each student briefly explaining what they can bring to the table.

That is, each student will pitch themselves to the class. Their goal is to answer the question: "Why should I hire you?"

Why

"Why should I hire you?" is a question your students will get in some way shape or form in every internship and job interview. Students need to learn to be able to advocate for themselves. And teams need to know what potential teammates bring to the table. Explain to your students that learning to pitch themselves is an important skill to develop and that this activity will give them practice doing so in a safe, supportive environment. You can talk a little bit about elevator pitches if you like by sharing and discussing this article:

- https://hbr.org/2018/10/the-art-of-the-elevator-pitch.

How

Have your students make a list of what assets they "bring to the table," including skills, talents, and experiences. I show a list of a variety of potential assets to help students think broadly about what they may offer a group. This helps head off the typical, "but I don't have anything to offer" complaint. Here's a list you can use. Feel free to build on it:

- Organization skills
- Writing and editing skills
- Blogging experience
- Video editing experience

- Videography
- Photography
- Creativity
- Leadership abilities
- Working with audio (recording, editing)
- Prior work, internship or other experience in public relations, social media, marketing, or related fields
- Willingness to learn new things
- Comfort with technology
- Dependability
- Image or video editing software (Photoshop, InDesign, Canva, etc.)
- Presentation skills
- Punctuality
- Good at working in teams

It is important that students understand that when they are pitching themselves, they're not just selling facts – they are telling a story and pitching an idea. I tell my students "Don't simply tell us facts about you. Sell us the idea of working with you." After the students have created their list, have them use that list to answer the question: What are the benefits to the listener? I tell my students to focus on the top reason or reasons that they think someone should hire them. I tell them to lead with that, and then to provide supporting evidence as necessary. For example, "I'm a team player with the experience to help this project succeed" can be followed with supporting points such as examples of how the person has worked effectively in teams and examples of how the person has relevant experience, such as internships. This approach is better than standing up and delivering a disconnected list of their accomplishments.

Do

Give your students 5 to 10 minutes to prepare their pitch. Their pitch will be no more than 30 seconds. If time is an issue, give students 15 seconds – shortening the time period helps the students boil down to the main point. When ready, go around the room and have each student stand up and give their pitch. Before doing so, tell your students to be thinking of the types of people and skills that they will want in their group. If students have an idea of the social media platform that they want to work with, tell them to keep an eye out for potential team members that may add value to their team.

You will be surprised at the array of talents, experiences, and knowledge that your students will share. Show support for your students by applauding them or giving a positive comment about something they share. Encourage your students to do this as well. In the fall of 2018, one student got very excited when he heard another student's pitch and said aloud, "Wow, I want to work with [name redacted]!" I believe this positive, sincere acknowledgment made the student feel good and showed the other students that such abilities were valued.

Drilldown: Group Checks and Balances

As we discussed in Chapter 1, there are challenges that come with asking students to work in teams. But I firmly believe that the positives to team projects outweigh the negatives. Here are some tools you can employ to maximize the likelihood that your students' "teamwork makes the dream work." Specifically, I will discuss team contracts, the right to fire team members, and team evaluations. Note that I use the terms team and group interchangeably.

Team Contracts

Team contracts are the first step to setting expectations. Contracts are a way of getting students to buy into the group because they empower the students to discuss and form the standards against which they wish to be judged. Said another way, the students in a team come together and decide on the rules that they expect everyone on the team to play by. Failure to play by those rules can result in a teammate getting a reduced grade on a project or getting fired (we will discuss firing of team members below). Having your students write a team contract also helps them understand one another's expectations and thereby the contract serves as a proactive tool that can help prevent miscommunications and disagreements as to what constitutes appropriate group norms.

What goes into a team contract:

1. **Names and contact information**: Here students decide how they wish to communicate. I find that students often prefer group chats using a messaging app.
2. **The dates students are available to meet outside of class:** By comparing schedules ahead of time, students find common ground meeting times that work for everyone. By prompting your students to compare schedules, you help reduce the common excuse of "I wasn't available when my team met."
3. **Team rules and expectations:** I tell my students that the rules they set in their contract serve as the basis for what they can use to request that a teammate gets a lower grade or to fire a teammate. These are the standards against which all teammates are to be held. For example, if the group expects that each member will always communicate if they have to miss a meeting, and one teammate does not comply with this expectation, then the team can take corrective action. On the other hand, a group has little recourse in the case that they made no expectations regarding missing meetings and communication because it would be

unfair to hold a teammate to a standard that was not set. In many ways, this essential step helps to mitigate the likelihood of miscommunication and thus group problems. It also is critical to team buy-in; without it, each members does not have a clear sense of what does or does not violate expectations.

Think of the team contract as a survival guide. Give your students 10 to 15 minutes to build their contract. I've provided a copy of my team contracts and ramifications activity in the chapter appendix. Encourage your students to discuss what frustrates them about group work before it becomes an issue. This open dialogue lets the students put their cards on the table. Next, tell them to find a reasonable way of avoiding those frustrations. I like to provide examples of team expectations, which you can see in the "Team Contract" activity sheet in the chapter appendix. Once your students have completed the contracts, collect them, photocopy them, and give one copy to each team member. I keep the original, signed contract for each group.

Team Evaluations

Now that team expectations have been set and teammates have bought in, students are able to evaluate their teammates. I plan team evaluations throughout the semester, such that teams will evaluate one another a few times. In my social media class, I do two team evaluations with each evaluation worth 9% of their total grade. I feel that having about one fifth of their grade come from their peers is reasonable in a class that relies heavily on group work. Note that everyone gets the same grade on the project (sans unusual circumstances which will be described in the section of firing teammates below), so the team evaluation is the 'hand that tips the scale' when it comes to balancing out grades.

I do one team evaluation after the first or second group assignment and the other at the end of the semester. However, team evaluations can be done at whatever frequency you feel is appropriate.

I suggest that you do not release team evaluation grades to students. This is important because if a student thought her peers would know how she evaluated them, the student may be less likely to be candid in her evaluation.

I have tried several different approaches to team evaluations, including combinations of both qualitative and quantitative measures. But, for me, nothing has performed as effectively as Michaelson's approach to team evaluations (Michaelson, Knight, & Fink, 2004)[7].

Students have a tendency to score all of their teammates well, probably

---

[7] Learn more about the Michaelson method and other methods of team-based learning here: http://tblc.roundtablelive.org/page-1032389. The Center for Teaching at Vanderbilt University offers more information about team-based learning and peer (e.g., team) evaluations https://cft.vanderbilt.edu/guides-sub-pages/team-based-learning/.

because they want to be a nice person or just don't want to think too hard about the evaluation process. This type of evaluation does not help you discern who really worked hard and who didn't.

In the Michaelson approach, the student evaluates everyone but himself. The student takes the total number of people in the group and subtracts himself. If there are five people total in the group, the number is four. There are 10 points per student to distribute. So, in our example, multiply the number of students that one student would evaluate in a group of five, which is four (everyone but himself), by 10. That is a total of 40 points.

The student must distribute those 40 points among his teammates. Yet there is a catch. He must give at least one student a score of nine or lower and he must give at least one student a score of 11 or higher. This forces the students to really think about who did the most work and who did the least. Giving points to one person is to take points away from someone else. This scarcity gets the students to take the evaluation seriously.

Chances are that your students won't be happy about this. They'll say, "Well that's not fair." So explain to them how and why it is fair. A person who did more work deserves a better grade. If students are able to evaluate each of their teammates independently, they tend to give inflated scores to everyone in their team which does not reflect the reality they experienced. Importantly, make a point to tell the students that by giving someone a nine they are not banishing that person to the Land of Bad Grades (I will explain why below).

In each example below, the team has four people in it. So each person is evaluating three other people.

If everyone did about the same work, students will score each other very closely:

John 11, Sally 10, Jim 9 (Jane is doing the evaluation)

But if someone was clearly doing a lot, or a little, it shows up:

John 7, Sally 10, Jim 13 (Jane is doing the evaluation)

Students are encouraged to explain their scores at the bottom of the evaluation sheet. Once you collect the evaluations, add up the scores from each evaluation within one group. Divide each student's score by the highest score. For example, imagine John got the highest score once all scores for his team were added up. His total was 28 points. Jim got a total of 22 points. So, John got an 100% (he did the most work, and went above and beyond others) and Jim gets 22/28=78%. In this way, students are compared in relation to the person who does the most work. The person who does a lot of extra work sets the bar high. Other students suffer if they also do not work hard. This is fairer to the student who does more of the work.

If the work is distributed fairly evenly, then everyone is probably happy and they scored everyone like this: John 11, Sally 10, Jim 9 (In fact, some very happy groups will conspire so that in the end everyone has the same score. I don't stop this).

In this case, let's say John has 33 (he got all 11s from the three people evaluating him). Jim ended up with 27 (three 9s, which is the lowest score possible if no one dipped below 9). He still got a B-, at 81.8%. It is very unlikely that one person gets all the 11s and one person gets all the 9s in a group like this. If the scores did fall this way, it is because the team is saying Jim did less work.

The math takes care of itself and what emerges is a clear picture of who really did the extra work and who did not. In the majority of cases, I let the math decide the students' grades on team evaluations. However, in some cases I take in other data points and use them to adjust team evaluation grades. Examples include my own observations of teams, if students in a team express concern over a teammate, or other issues.

Firing Teammates and Other Safeguards

Students have a right to expect great work from their peers. They should be empowered to hold their peers accountable. They should be accountable to their peers. That's my philosophy. With that in mind, I allow students to fire a teammate who is not living up to the group's expectations per the team contract. Of course, there are other circumstances where one could warrant firing a teammate and I have had those, but I try to stick to the contracts as much as possible.

It may seem harsh to let students fire other students. But consider what would happen if you repeatedly broke the rules at your job or did not do what was expected of you. You would be reprimanded, and if the behavior did not improve, you would likely find yourself looking for a new job.

By empowering students to be able to fire teammates, I believe that students are being given the opportunity to learn to advocate for their interests in a professional manner when the actions of others adversely affect them in a work environment.

At the start of the semester, I briefly explain the process of how to fire a teammate which I will outline below.

First, set a deadline in the semester that students have to first issue someone an official warning before they can fire the person. Another way to do this is to require students to give a teammate a warning with enough time in advance (say, two weeks) that the student may correct the action.

A warning is a written complaint that a team files with the professor. It serves to officially put a student on notice that if they do not change their behavior, then they will likely be fired. The warning usually solves the problem without the drastic measure of firing the student because it gives the warned student a chance to make changes. I've found that, just like in most conflicts, people often just want the other person to know how they feel.

With the warning system, the grievance has been aired and everyone in the group is aware that the warning exists.

In order for a team to be able to issue a warning, the majority of the remaining teammates must agree to issue the warning. So, if there are four students in a group, two of the remaining three students would have to vote in favor of issuing the warning.

Requiring the majority of teammates to agree to a warning helps reduce 'he said, she said' scenarios where two people are simply not getting along and one is using the group as an outlet for what is really an interpersonal conflict. However, it could result in a student feeling unfairly targeted. In the chapter appendix, you will find a copy of the Team Member Warning form.

Once a warning has been issued, if the team decides that the warned student hasn't improved, then they can file a Petition to Fire A Team Member. The process is similar to what is used in the warning. The majority has to vote for the firing. A specific reason has to be given as to why they are electing to fire this teammate. I make the final decision to ensure the cause is justifiable. In the chapter appendix, you will find a copy of the Petition to Fire A Team Member form.

Once a student gets fired, that student keeps all grades that they earned while working with their former team. The student has the choice to either join a new group or work on any remaining assignments on their own. If the student wants to join another group, I assist them in finding a new group. I leave the decision to the group they are seeking to join as to whether they want to accept the new person.

By making team firings a procedure-driven exercise, I believe it removes some of the emotion, potential perceived favoritism, and conflict from the situation. Because it involves effort to fire someone, teammates are not casually firing one. The process fairly protects all teammates.

It is often the case that students will not want to fire others as that is a dramatic step. This is especially true if you work in a small department where students will be seeing each other in future classes. But knowing that this 'nuclear option' is available gives teams a sense of empowerment and helps motivate unmotivated students.

In this drill down section, we have discussed three tools that you can employ to help teamwork go smoothly: Team contracts, team evaluations and the ability to fire teammates. Whatever tools you use, remember that "empowered students do powerful things." Take the time to plan how you will empower your students to succeed in group work.

Documentary Recommendation

I encourage you to assign a documentary for your students to watch for homework during the first week of classes. It will help you contextualize the class and give the students some food for thought as they head into the semester. For the past few years, I have shown the PBS Frontline documentary *Generation Like* (Koughan & Rushkoff, 2014)[8]. I recommend showing this documentary because it reveals how companies use social media to create groundswell, while questioning the ramifications of social media on society.

Recommended Readings and More

Readings

Dietrich, G. (2018, January 4). PR pros must embrace the PESO model. Spin Sucks. Retrieved from https://spinsucks.com/communication/pr-pros-must-embrace-the-peso-model/.

Gallo, C. (2018, October 3). The art of the elevator pitch. *Harvard Business Review*. Retrieved from https://hbr.org/2018/10/the-art-of-the-elevator-pitch.

What is content marketing? (n.d.). Content Marketing Institute. Retrieved from https://contentmarketinginstitute.com/what-is-content-marketing/.

Television

Koughan, F. & Rushkoff, D. (Writers), Mangini, T. (Director). (February 18, 2014). Generation Like [Television series episode]. In D. Fanning (Producer). *Frontline*. Boston, Massachusetts: WGBH/Boston.

---

8 While Generation Like first broadcast in 2014, students continue to tell me that the larger issues discussed in this documentary are still relevant . As of the fall 2018, my students encouraged me to show the documentary the following year. For more info about this documentary and why I use it, please see this blog post I wrote: http://mattkushin.com/2015/09/14/social-media-documentary-recommendation-generation-like/. You can stream Generation Like through the PBS website: https://www.pbs.org/wgbh/frontline/film/generation-like/.

Chapter 3 Appendix

The Team Contract Activity Sheet

Team Contract and Ramifications

The team contract aims to promote academic integrity among team members. Here are the rules: You must meet the contract or face the consequences decided upon by the team, and any established by the professor (i.e., in the syllabus). You will be held accountable to these standards. Throughout the semester, you will conduct an assessment of your teammates' work in this class.

Recourse Against Unproductive Teammates
1) **Students With Multiple Absences** - Your participation in your team is an integral part of this class. Students who have four unexcused absences will receive a letter grade reduction; students with five will fail the class.
2) **Requesting Grade Reduction on Unproductive Teammates** - If a majority of the students in your team are dissatisfied with the commitment of a team member on a project but do not want to fire them from the team, the majority can request that the teammate receives a grade reduction. The team can recommend a percent reduction. Ex: 50% off the team grade. The professor will consider their request and appropriate action will be taken.
3) **Firing Team Members -** After a few weeks into the semester, the professor will allow your team to fire any member whom you feel is not fulfilling their obligations. A member must be warned first before they can be fired (see "Issue a Team Warning" document). Fired members can either 1) join another team, 2) work on their own. Members fired from a team will retain all grades they earned prior to being fired. They will, however, receive a reduction in their overall participation grade and will lose all credit on team evaluations for projects completed. For more information about rules and procedures for firing team members – see the "Petition to Fire Team Member" document. In consultation with the professor, extreme circumstances of unproductive members may warrant the firing of a group member without a warning being filed first.

Instructions
Work as a group to complete the below tasks. Turn in your signed sheet. It will be photocopied. Each teammate will get a copy. The professor will keep the original. There are 3 parts to the assignment:

    1. Contact Info: Enter each group member's name, email and phone #.

    2. Availability: Discuss your schedules and identify common times your group is available to meet.

    3. Expectations for group work: Identify 4-5 expectations for each group member, and any consequences.

Sample expectations:

Sample 1

We agree to:

1. Make sure that when we miss class that we contact the others in our group.
2. That we will work on every group assignment collaboratively.
3. Group members have the right, by consensus, to approach a group member who is not participating and ask them to leave the group at his/her loss.
4. Everyone needs to be at every meeting. If you are not able to make it to a meeting, be sure to tell your group members ahead of time with the above contact information.

Sample 2

1. If I am unable to attend class, I will make it my personal responsibility to get any and all notes from my group.
2. Under any and all circumstances, I will get what work I am allotted to do, done and turned in on time.
3. The time and place of group meetings shall be agreed upon unanimously within our group.
4. I will be in attendance, and arrive promptly, for every group meeting. Should an emergency arise that prevents me from attending a group meeting, I will notify my group members immediately.
5. I will do my share of the group work, there will never be an occasion where one group member does all of the work nor will there be a time when a group member does none of the work.

Team contract

Group Availability:

Name	Contact Info	Availability

Group Expectations: Write your expectations below.

We agree to adhere to the above group expectations. Failure to do so may result in penalty decided upon by the group, and any established by the professor via the course policies.

Signatures:

The Team Members Warning Form

Issue a Team Warning Form

As discussed on the "Team Contract," this document outlines rules and procedures for issuing a team member a warning.

About:
1. This form issues a warning to a team member who is not completing their fair share of the team's work for team assignments, as determined by the rest of the group.
2. To fire a member, you must have first issued a team warning and have that team warning on file with the professor.
3. However, just because a warning is issued, does not mean a team member will be fired from a group. It is just a warning. Its purpose is to inform the member that they must improve their work or they may be fired from the group.
4. Receiving a warning does not hurt a students' grade.

Procedure:
To issue a warning, the following is needed:
1. Majority vote from those members who would remain in the team after the termination of the fired member(s). Vote must be documented via signature on a copy of your warning to fire member.
2. A Warning must be written and submitted to the professor by the deadline. The warning should include a rationale. For example, how is the student causing a substantial distress to the team that is preventing the team from performing at its best?

What Happens Next?
The professor keeps a copy of the warning.

The professor scans the warning and emails the scan and/or hands a hard copy of the warning to the student as the student deserves to know why they are being warned.

The Petition to Fire a Team Member Form

Petition to Fire Team Member

As discussed on the "Team Contract," this document outlines rules and procedures for firing team members.

Procedure:
To fire a member of your team, you should:
1. Have issued a warning to the team member by the deadline, adhering to the "Team Member Warning" procedures on the file: "Issue a Team Member Warning."
    - Note: In rare cases, the team warning requirement can be overridden. Discuss with the professor.

You need:
1. Majority vote from those members who would remain in your team after the termination of the fired member. Vote must be documented via signature on a copy of the petition to fire member.
2. A petition to fire the member must be written and submitted to the professor, generally by the deadline to fire members unless the issue is first discussed with the professor. The petition should document your reason(s) for petitioning to fire the member. For example, how are they causing a substantial distress to the team that is preventing the team from performing at its best?

What happens next?
1. The professor will review your petition and if it is reasonable will grant it. Then, the professor will inform the fired members.
2. A copy of your petition will be made available to the fired member(s) upon request.

Remember:
1. Fired members can either 1) join another team, 2) be forced to work on their own (If you are fired from your team – you are not doomed to fail. But it should be a wakeup call!) Members fired from a team will retain all grades they earned prior to being fired.
2. Fired members will receive a reduction in their overall participation grade and will lose all credit on team evaluations for projects completed.

CHAPTER 4. UNIT 2. SOCIAL MEDIA LISTENING

The second unit of the semester introduces students to listening. It provides students with an opportunity to begin developing social media listening skills, which they will build upon throughout the semester.

Now that students are familiar with the main thrust of the semester and have formed their teams, it is time to get into the exciting stuff. We start with a unit on social media listening.

Teaching your students about social listening is a great way to help them begin to understand the strategic use of social media across many related business functions such as public relations, customer relations, sales, and marketing. Remember, your students are likely pros at using social media for personal purposes. But most of them will have little understanding or experience in the professional applications of social media. If you teach public relations, then you are probably already emphasizing the importance of listening to, and understanding, your audiences. Social listening on social media is merely an outgrowth of that. Think of it as a tool for getting to know the audiences your client wants to have a relationship with.

In this unit, we will look at what social media listening is, why it is important, and how to do it. We will also introduce the social media audit assignment, which is the first assignment related to the semester social media project. This unit can be completed in three class periods if the class is taught two days a week with each class period lasting one hour and fifteen minutes. However, I suggest extending it into four days by giving your students a dedicated social listening activities lab day. This will let them practice social listening through an in-class activity based around the below-discussed material.

Suggested Schedule: Weeks 2 and 3

1. Day 3: An Overview of Social Media Listening
2. Day 4 (optional): Social Listening Activities Lab Day
3. Day 5: The Social Media Audit
4. Day 6: Social Media Audit Lab Day

Unit Learning Objectives

1. Introduce students to social listening and why it's important.
2. Teach students the skills to perform social media listening using various tools.
3. Introduce students to social media audits and why they are performed.
4. Prepare students to apply their social listening skills to conduct a social media audit using their critical and analytical thinking abilities.

The What, Why, How, Do, Reflect

Below, I break down each learning objective above into its appropriate stages within the What, Why, How, Do, Reflect (WWHDR) framework. You will note that we are dealing with a lesson unit, so some objectives do not contain each stage of the WWHDR framework because the learning objectives build upon each other.

Learning Objective 1: Introduce Social Listening

What

The first step to building a relationship is to get to know the other person. We listen to what the person has to say, find out about their interests and disinterests, and get a sense of who the person is and how the person talks. The same applies to understanding any public or organization we want to build a relationship with.

Social media listening is an important form of research that is used to assess the social media landscape as it relates to a brand. In her book, *Social Media Campaigns: Strategies for Public Relations and Marketing*, Carolyn Mae Kim writes that the goal is to "identify what conversations are taking place on social media that may be relevant to the brand, who is having those conversations, and ways that the organization might engage with that dialogue" (p. 32).

Create a brief lecture introducing students to social media listening. Social media textbooks break down the subsets that comprise social media listening such as monitoring relevant keywords, conducting audience analysis, examining community engagement with the audience, and monitoring competitors. Below, I will offer a cursory explanation of monitoring relevant keywords, assessing sentiment scores, and conducting an audience analysis. If these are topics you are not familiar with, I recommend the textbooks written by Carolyn Mae Kim, Karen Freberg and Keith A. Quesenberry for detailed discussions. I've cited each in the Recommended Readings and More section at the end of this chapter. I also encourage you to explore this great slide deck by Kelli Burns on social media analytics which also covers these concepts:

- https://www.canva.com/design/DADIUKfiayc/N3lHWoaekp8C FICzP2sL7Q/view

Monitoring Relevant Keywords

Monitoring relevant keywords is the process of identifying words and phrases relevant to your client and actively monitoring their use online. First, brainstorm a list of relevant keywords. You can also discover relevant keywords by searching keywords you already know about, such as a brand's product, and looking for other, related keywords. Discoveries may include colloquialisms brand fans use to refer to your client's products.

Here are some more examples: If your client sells smartwatches, what are some words or phrases relevant to that market? There may be brands, product names, important features, and the like, that are relevant. While brand and product names may be easy to think of, there are other important keywords to think of. For example, if your client sells automobiles, what features do consumers look for when searching for a new automobile? This might include gas mileage, safety ratings, or even the number of cup holders. You should monitor the conversation around their competitors as well. Organizations will also want to monitor the names of high-level employees in their own company, slogans and taglines relevant to their brand, and keywords relevant to advertising or public relations campaigns. It may be helpful to think of keyword monitoring as the lead into social media listening more broadly.

Students can use social media listening tools to generally monitor the conversation happening around the class client and its competitors. Start doing this by identifying the appropriate keywords (as discussed above) to monitor on relevant social media platforms. This lets you hone in on the right online conversations relevant to your client. Thus, if your client is your academic department, then relevant keywords will include your department name – including all possible spellings and nicknames (e.g., XYZ University Comm Department, XYZ University Communication Department, XYZ Comm Department, XYZ Communication Department, etc.) -, any hashtags your department uses, the names of relevant faculty, clubs, or organizations, and other terms relevant to your specific academic department.

Negative keywords are keywords that you want the search to exclude. Negative keywords may include names, towns, mascots, and the like that are similar to your client and thus may end up as false positives in your search results.

You may also want to have your students monitor the larger conversation around your client by brainstorming keywords around it. By monitoring the online conversation, students can stay abreast of trends, threats, and opportunities. They can get a sense of how people feel about the client, how people feel about its competitors, how people are reacting to public relations or marketing efforts, and more. Further, your students can see what accounts are posting about your client the most, what hashtags are being used the most, what keywords are being used related to your client, what the sentiment score is related to your client's posts, and more.

Sentiment Scores

If you are not familiar with the concept of online sentiment, here is a quick explanation. Online sentiment is the valence around a topic. A sentiment score is the sentiment rating related to that specific keyword for a given search timeframe. Let's say you perform a search for a set of keywords about your academic department and the search spans a timeframe of two weeks. While each social listening platform has its own way of scoring sentiment, you may get a sentiment score delivered as a percentage. If 60% of your search results contain positive sentiment, then your sentiment score would be 60% positive. An example positive post is, "I love my classes in the XYZ communication department." A negative post may read, "I hate my classes in the XYZ communication department." A post that is scored as neutral may read, "I take classes in the XYZ communication department." How sentiment is calculated is beyond the scope of this book. But it is important to know that sentiment scoring is widely critiqued for being inaccurate. You may find that the sentiment for your keyword search is 60% negative. But, by drilling down into the actual posts, you may find that many posts were incorrectly coded as negative. This is because the computational scoring that underpins sentiment analysis faces limitations due to the complexities of human communication which often require a complete understanding of context to infer intended meaning (Dalisay, Kushin & Yamamoto, 2017)[9]. A simple example of this is the use of sarcasm when the words used and the intended meaning are often in contrast with one another.

Audience Analysis

An audience analysis is used to build a prototype, sometimes called an audience persona, of the audience (aka, public) in question. This audience persona contains both demographic and behavioral information, or psychographics, to create a fictionalized profile of the ideal member of the target audience. It is helpful to have this audience persona in mind when crafting a social media plan because it humanizes the target audience. It helps us understand where they are coming from, what motivates them, and how they think.

---

[9] To learn more about sentiment analysis, how it works, and its limitations, please see Dalisay, Kushin and Yamamoto (2017) in the reference section.

An audience persona can be built, in part, by researching the online profiles and behaviors of people who fit the target audience.

An audience analysis, then, is a way of getting to know the target audience(s). But when looked at from a wider lens, it can also be a way to get to know more about one or both of two important audiences: Who is talking about your client online, and who your client wishes was talking about them online. Hopefully, these two audiences are the same. But, you may find that they are not. You may also find that the people who are talking about your client are not who your client thought was talking about them. To get to know who is talking about your client online, your students can monitor the online conversation around the client and see who those people are, where they hang out online, what they like, what they dislike, how they talk, etc.

To learn more about a target audience, seek out people who fill the client's target audience and expand from there. For example, if the target audience is U.S.-based teenagers who play lacrosse and who may be interested in consuming plant-based protein as a workout supplement, your students could start by exploring the online spaces that interest this audience such as Instagram or YouNow. The target audience could be found through search on those platforms. From there, your students can begin to scour the online profiles of persons who fit the target demographic. They can use this information to build an audience persona. With a little investigating, quite a bit can be learned about people just by looking at their public profiles.

In Learning Objective 2 below, I will provide an activity for students to conduct an audience analysis.

Why

A relatable and fun reason for why we do social listening is provided in the Why section of Learning Objective 3 below when I discuss social media audits. For now, it is sufficient to explain to your students that listening to the online conversation is a core practice used by agencies and brands big and small to understand existing perceptions. If you teach public relations, you can note that public relations is about building mutually beneficial relationships and listening is a key component of any relationship.

You can stoke your students' curiosity about social listening with a brief prompt. Ask them to imagine that they represent a popular brand, say Nike or Starbucks. If the students could be a fly on the wall in a conversation that was happening about that brand, what would they want to know? Another way to put this question is to ask your students: What type of questions would any brand want to know about their audience?

You might get answers such as, 'Who is talking about our brand?' 'What do they like?' 'How do they spend their time?' 'What do they do for a living?' 'What are they saying?' 'What are they saying about our competitors?' 'Who are they talking to about our brand?' There are many questions we could want to know the answer to, so help your students along if they are having a hard time thinking of them.

I recommend you assign the following article to your students to read by Fournier, Quelch and Rietveld titled "To get more out of social media, think like an anthropologist:"

- https://hbr.org/2016/08/to-get-more-out-of-social-media-think-like-an-anthropologist.

In Learning Objective 2 below, we will cover specific applications of several subsets of social media listening discussed in the What section above. In so doing, your students will get the opportunity to move beyond this wider conversation about what we would like to monitor and dig into specific questions that I like to have my students monitor around our academic department.

Learning Objective 2: Teach Social Media Listening Tools

In the below section, I will cover three activities that you can have your students complete to begin learning to use social media listening tools to: 1) Do keyword research, 2) answer some common social listening questions, and 3) conduct an audience analysis. Each of these activities is done in the student groups that you have set up – the groups that will later be in charge of your client's different social media platforms.

What

There are many social media listening software applications. Many, if not most, of these applications are paid services. Agencies pay big bucks to use them and that can make them cost-prohibitive for most universities. However, there are a host of free tools available. In addition, some companies offer free or discounted access to their software for use in the university classroom. Other companies offer free trials.

You can find an often-updated and thorough list of social listening software, and social media tools more broadly, on Keith Quesenberry's website. He has organized these tools into categories:

- http://www.postcontrolmarketing.com/337-tools-resources-improve-social-media-strategy-2019/.

The tools we are going to talk about fall into social media monitoring and metrics tools. However, we will talk in Chapter 7 about measuring social media metrics, the process of monitoring engagement with your brand's social media accounts. For now, we are focusing just on social media listening and software that enables it.

Below is a list of free tools or tools that have free versions which your students can use to perform social media listening. The trouble with free tools is that they tend to transform and take on new shapes in time. What is free today is soon to be behind a paywall, or even worse, no longer exist. Therefore, I cannot guarantee that these services are still free by the time you read this. During the time that I wrote this book, several companies that were providing professors and students with free access to their software closed or changed their university programs.

Name	Learn more about their university program
Hootsuite Social Media Dashboard	https://hootsuite.com/pages/landing/student-program
Meltwater Media Intelligence Software	This program has closed to future sign ups as of spring 2019. It will be discontinued at the end of 2019 for all participating universities.
HubSpot	https://academy.hubspot.com/education-partner-program
Microsoft Social Engagement (part of the Microsoft Business Applications Academic Community software suite) [10]	https://dynamics.microsoft.com/en-us/academic/

The lack of access to the social media listening and analytics software programs presents a struggle for educators. While a few universities have the budget to pay for their students to have access to software like Brandwatch, Talkwalker, or Nuvi, the majority of professors and programs are not able to afford these products.

Yet, my concerns were alleviated by a conversation I had in June 2019 with the social intelligence lead for a Fortune 500 company. During a visit to this company, another professor and I expressed the challenge we face in providing our students with access to professional social media listening software. We shared our fear that we are unable to adequately prepare our students for industry jobs.

His response?

He told us that he was not concerned about whether incoming hires had used a particular software package or not. He could train new hires on the

---

[10] In January 2019, Microsoft announced that Microsoft Social Engagement is being discontinued. A new product, Microsoft Dynamics 365 AI for Market Insights, which will combine web and social insights, has been created. At the time of publication, it is unclear as to whether it will be part of the academic alliance program. Also, in march, 2019, Microsoft announced that they were renaming the education partnership program through which Microsoft Social Engagement is made available. The partnership program was renamed from Microsoft Dynamics Academic Alliance program to Microsoft Business Applications Academic Community.

software his company used in just a few days. He was more concerned that new hires had critical thinking skills and experience analyzing and interpreting social data. In fact, he did not want his team to rely just on the data extracted from a social media dashboard. He wanted them to go beyond the trends and quantitative data on social media dashboards and dig into the qualitative data: The actual conversations that are happening on platforms like Twitter, Facebook, Reddit, and others. He suggested that students be able to dig into relevant conversations and answer questions such as "what are people excited about and what are they afraid of?"

Gathering and reading the data is not a problem. The Fortunate 500 company this person works for uses several enterprise-level software programs to gather and slice social media data and display it in an easily digestible format. He wants employees that can tell him what to do with the data.

Social media listening software is glossy and enticing. It is the shiny object that I'll admit I can't pull my eyes away from. It is fun to play with and certainly makes life easier. It is a great recruiting tool for our programs. While as professors, we may get caught up with a feeling that our students need access to this software, that may not be true. We should remind ourselves that it is the skills and abilities that we are teaching our students that translate to the industry. If we focus on the skills and abilities, then free tools can do the trick.

The social listening exercise discussed later in this chapter was designed around Meltwater Media Intelligence software. However, I have conducted this exercise with Microsoft Social Engagement as well as the free tools listed directly below; no expensive software needed.

Free tools that you can use to perform the below exercises are:

- BuzzsSumo monitoring tool - https://app.buzzsumo.com/alerts/about
- BuzzSumo trending tool - https://app.buzzsumo.com/research/trending
- Instagram Search – https://instagram.com
- Sentiment Viz - https://www.csc2.ncsu.edu/faculty/healey/tweet_viz/tweet_app/
- Social Mention - http://socialmention.com
- Social Searcher - https://www.social-searcher.com
- Tweetdeck - https://tweetdeck.twitter.com/
- Twitter Advanced Search – https://twitter.com/search-advanced

Paid tools with free trials you can use to perform the below exercises:

- Keyhole - https://keyhole.co/
- Mention Mapp - https://mentionmapp.com/
- Mentionlytics - https://www.mentionlytics.com/
- Mediatoolkit - https://www.mediatoolkit.com/
- Sprout Social - https://sproutsocial.com/features/social-media-listening/

- Talkwalker - https://www.talkwalker.com/

Why

We have already talked about why in the learning objective above and we will talk about why further below. So, let's move on.

How, Do and Reflect

Keywords Activity

The below activity offers your students an opportunity to identify keywords. The purpose of this activity is to generate a list of relevant keywords that can then be programmed into the social listening software you are using.

Start your students with a quick primer on Boolean search. Simply put, Boolean search is a way to add specificity to an online search. For example, imagine your university's sports team name is a fairly common sports team name such the "Tigers." Wikipedia currently lists 26 college and professional teams that are named "Tigers" in the United States alone ("Tigers (sports teams)," 2018). This does not include youth and high school teams named "Tigers" or international sports teams named "Tigers." So, a search on Twitter for "Tigers" will produce a ton of irrelevant results. Using basic Boolean search, here are a few ways to filter out these false positives.

You can combine these operators to produce your search phrase. For example: "Bayou AND Bengals NOT Cincinnati" will produce search results that include the phrase Bayou Bengals (the nickname for the LSU Tigers) and will not include any reference to Cincinnati (home to the Cincinnati Bengals).

Note that Twitter's advanced search tool enables you to perform these functions without the use of Boolean search operators and modifiers because it creates textboxes specific to the related search, such as "All of these words," "This exact phrase," "Any of these words," and "None of these words."

I encourage you to read and share the following articles with your students. These articles provide more depth of how Boolean search can be used to add greater specificity to a search and thus to make it more likely that the results you will get from a search are the results you are looking for:

- http://booleanblackbelt.com/2008/12/basic-boolean-search-operators-and-query-modifiers-explained/
- https://www.meltwater.com/uk/blog/boolean-media-monitoring/.

Now, put your students to task building a keyword list.

First, if you haven't yet, provide some possible topics relevant to your client (product names, persons, competitors, etc.). Then, have student teams use these topics to brainstorm keywords relevant to your client. Then, set these teams loose on your client's website, social media, and the like to find more possible keywords. Next, have them do some searching around on Twitter or Instagram for relevant keywords using their newfound Boolean skills.

Boolean Operator or Modifier	What it does	Examples
AND	Narrows search so that it must contain all keywords	▪ Tigers AND Princeton ▪ Tigers AND Louisiana AND State
OR	Broadens search to include possibility of one or more terms in search.	▪ Lions OR Tigers OR Bears ▪ Tigers OR Bengals
NOT	Eliminates keywords from a search so that your search will show the keyword you want	▪ Tigers NOT LSU ▪ Tigers NOT Lions
Parentheses	If multiple ORs exist in your search, put them in parenthesis to ensure the search executes correctly.	▪ Tigers NOT (LSU OR Cincinnati) ▪ Tigers NOT (Lions OR Bears)
Asterisk	Saves time by producing search results with any ending to a root word.	▪ Sport* Note: This will return sports, sporting, sport, sported, etc.
Quotation Marks	Narrow search to exact phrases so that all results show the exact words in order.	▪ "LSU Tigers" Note: This will return results such as "LSU Tigers played today," rather than all possible words in the search but not in the exact order specified such as "LSU is the home of Tigers stadium."

Have the students try different Boolean searches and refine them to add accuracy and reduce false positives. Keep in mind that searches that work on one platform, say Instagram, may not work on another platform due to differences in culture and convention across social media platforms. Further, keep in mind that it may be useful to have a few different searches that are relevant to your client. For example, you may want to have a search set up for posts related to your academic department and another search set up for posts related to your university at large, and yet another search set up for posts related to specific mentions of the TV station, radio station, newspaper, or other organization associated with your department.

If you want to take this activity to the next level, you can have your students use a social media dashboard such as Hootsuite or Tweetdeck to set up a few searches in order to monitor the conversation on social media platforms such as Twitter or Instagram. If you are not familiar with social media dashboards, these tools enable users the ability to monitor several social media streams at once in a single platform. Usually, the social media streams are organized into columns in a single browser window. These tools are great for quickly monitoring the online conversation as well as for posting to social media from a single tool. While Tweetdeck is free and only works for Twitter, many paid tools, such as Hootsuite, enable users to post to and monitor the conversation across an array of social media platforms[11]. Such paid tools often provide metric reports, such as reports on user engagement with a social media account.

The benefit of using a social media dashboard is that once keyword searches are set up your students will be able to log back in throughout the semester to quickly monitor the conversation happening around your client.

For a reflection exercise, have your student teams compare their searches with each other, exploring both the search parameters and the results.

Social Media Listening Activity

In the keyword search exercise above, I spoke about monitoring the social media conversation and how this can be done through tools such as Twitter search as well as through social media dashboards such as Tweetdeck and Hootsuite.

Before we get into the below exercise, I want to articulate a distinction that I make between social media monitoring and social media listening.

Social media monitoring is the process of actively following a real-time stream of posts that result from a keyword search. In other words, it is about monitoring an ongoing conversation the way you might listen to two friends talking. Often, several streams are evaluated concurrently, possibly across several social media platforms. The purpose is to scan the current online conversation of interest. Social media dashboards are often used for this purpose. Social media monitoring enables the user to stay abreast of many live conversations at once and quickly participate in those conversations.

Social media listening is the process of gathering analytics about social media conversations that are of interest, often in real time. The purpose is to quickly analyze large sets of data pulled from keyword searches in order to extract insights. These tools produce visual representations of search results so that the user can quickly digest large sets of data. The user can then drill down into these visual representations to get a more fine-grained look at data of interest. Insights may include information about trends across time,

---

[11] Hootsuite offers free access to their software through a university program. See the software list earlier in this chapter.

volume or location. Insights may also include comparisons between times, locations, search parameters, etc. Insights may also include summaries of which accounts post the most for a given search, which terms are most commonly used related to a given search, or what the sentiment score for a search is. Tools such as Meltwater Media Intelligence Software, Microsoft Social Engagement, Social Searcher, and many others are often used to perform this task. Social media listening enables the user to see the big picture around the online conversation.

Now that we have that squared away, let's move on to the social media listening activity.

To set up this activity, identify a well-known brand that you want your students to investigate. The purpose of this exercise is to get students comfortable with using social media listening software and to help them begin to discover the rich array of information that can be gleaned with some purposive social media listening (They will do more advanced things with social listening when we get into monitoring your class client's content in Chapter 7). This exercise is even more interesting if you can identify a brand that has recently received a lot of buzz online, such as a company that has faced some controversy, created a bold conversation-starting campaign, launched a new product, or is otherwise the focus of much attention. For example, in Fall 2018, we chose Nike because of the timely release of the Nike advertisement featuring Colin Kaepernick. This ad received a strong reaction from the public. However, you do not need to pick a brand in the media spotlight for this activity to work.

Here's the scenario: Tell your students that the agency they work for was recently hired by the brand you chose. The agency they work for is going to represent this brand on social media. To get started, you, the team lead, want the students, your direct reports, to spend some time getting to know the conversation around the brand online.

Tell the students that there are specific questions you want them to explore. Use the activity sheet for the social media listening activity in the chapter appendix. That activity sheet contains the list of questions that you will want your students to answer. Recall, that I wrote these questions to be answered using the Meltwater Media Intelligence Software. Depending on what software you use, you can modify the questions to ensure that your students can answer them with the software at hand. Feel free to add your own questions.

Of the free tools listed in this chapter, I like Social Searcher (https://social-searcher.com) for social media listening. Students can create a free account which allows up to 100 real-time searchers per day. Once a search is performed, students can click the "detailed statistics" button to see post timelines, post volume by social network, posts by day of the week, hashtags used, sentiment scores, top users, keywords, and more.

You will first need to show your students how to use the software before turning them loose to work on this exercise. Importantly, be sure to show them the necessary steps to perform the queries needed to answer the questions. If the software has training videos, such as Meltwater does, assign your students to complete the training videos as homework before this day in class. To do this, you will of course need to first familiarize yourself with the software you are using. But the trouble with doing this is, if you are like me and do much of your course prep in the summer, when it comes time to teach these skills, you might forget some of the steps needed to answer the questions in the worksheet yourself. Thus, you may find it helpful while you are learning the software to create a lab guide – a document that contains key steps students will need for using a particular piece of software. Lab guides are visual guides that help students answer the questions on the worksheet[12]. That way, you can share the lab guide alongside the questions from the activity and point the students to the lab guide if they need help. An added benefit is that you can quickly review the lab guide before class to refresh on the software.

Have the students work on the activity on computers and go around the room and offer guidance.

Upon completion, spend a little time offering your students the opportunity to reflect upon their findings. The reflection portion of this activity is simple. As a class, have your groups share their findings. Look for cases of disagreement between groups and ask students why those cases might exist. A reason might be that students used different search terms and thus found different things, a la the keyword search exercise above. So, ask them what search terms they were using when they set up their search. This is an important topic to help them consider, because they need to be aware that the keywords they are using to cast their search affect the outcomes they find. Point out cases where two groups found dissimilar things. Ask your students how they can use the knowledge they now have gained. For example, play the role of team lead in this exercise and ask your students what they think you should know about the conversation online. Ask them how your agency could use this information to build a stronger relationship with the target audience. Ask your students what issues they see popping up that management needs to know about. Or, ask them what advice they would give to help your agency create content that would better resonate with the target audience. Ask them how the client could use this information to better serve their customers. The point is to get students thinking about how they can analyze, evaluate and apply the information they learned to make actionable decisions.

<u>Audience Analysis Activity</u>

There are many ways to tackle an audience analysis. This activity will

---

12 Learn more about lab guides and how I create mine here: http://mattkushin.com/2013/10/07/spice-up-your-handouts-with-multimedia-lab-guides/

allow your students to use the social media listening tools they have available to them to build an audience persona. Recall that an audience persona is a fictionalized person used to represent your target audience. However, this fictionalized person is created from real data and research.

Going into this exercise, you should have some idea of who your client's target audience is. The purpose of the audience persona is to focus or refine the target audience. Because your class is most likely taking on your academic department as a client, there are a few potential target audiences you can think of. They may include:

1. Current students – Students currently enrolled as majors or minors in your department.
2. Potential students – These may be incoming freshmen and transfers from other universities or other departments at your university.
3. Students' parents – After all, they have a big impact on a student's decision to attend your university or continue attending it.
4. The wider university community – They have a vested interest in your success.
5. The community where your university is situated - They might like to know about all the awesome things you're doing.

For this exercise, have your students pick current students or potential students as these audiences are most likely your primary audiences, whereas students' parents, the university community, and the community in which your university is situated are secondary audiences.

Tell your students that they will use this audience persona as part of their strategic brief assignment which you will be assigning soon (I discuss the strategic brief assignment in the next chapter).

Using one of the search services discussed previously, have your students conduct a social search on the target audience. Have a conversation with your students about what keywords to use to do this search. For example, if the audience persona is going to be about current students in your academic department, then searches surrounding your department social media are a good start to learn about follower demographics, psychographics, and behaviors.

If you are at a regional university and looking for prospective students, searches surrounding the university at large as well as local and regional high schools may be a start.

Your students probably have a good sense of where to find other current students or potential students online because they are closely associated with those populations.

Keep in mind that your students will already have assumptions about what a current student thinks because they are a current student and they might not readily look beyond their own perspectives and opinions. So remind them that you, the professor, are interested in what the students in your class think as a start, but that you want external data to bolster those claims and to help move beyond biases. Screenshots are an effective tool for showing evidence of what the students find and they can be easily dumped into Google Docs or Microsoft Word.

Once the search is up and running, have your students comb through the profiles of people who appear to fit your target audience. Keep in mind that there are likely many false positives in your search results, so combing through is necessary to find people that, based on information shared in their profile, demonstrate that they fit the target audience. Have your students extract information from the profiles and social media posts of people who fit into your target audience. Embedded in this content is information about their likes, dislikes, ambitions, current school or occupational statuses, etc.

Give the students about 15 or 20 minutes to complete this task. Walk around the room and check in with students, asking them to show you what they are finding. Ask them to synthesize the disparate pieces of evidence from profiles and social media posts made by people in their target audience. Once the students have amassed this evidence, tell each group to put their heads together and build an audience persona using the audience persona activity sheet in the chapter appendix.

Upon completion, have a reflection conversation with your students. Discuss what they found. Ask them to explain why they made the choices they did and how they think this information may be valuable as they move forward planning social media content in future assignments.

An alternative activity, and one I do in my strategic campaigns class, is to use the Facebook Audience Insights tool to have students create an audience persona based on summative data and percentages provided by Facebook Audience Insights[13]. In short, the purpose of this activity is for students to use the data they can obtain about their target audience through Facebook Audience Insights in order to create an audience persona[14]. You can use Facebook Audience Insights persona activity coupled with the audience persona activity to complete this task (both activities are in the chapter appendix). There is a great tutorial by MOZ on how to do this which includes screenshots. I encourage you to check it out if you want to go this route:

- https://moz.com/blog/facebook-insights-create-audience-personas-budget.

SocialMediaExaminer has a similar step-by-step guide:

- https://www.socialmediaexaminer.com/how-to-develop-buyer-personas-using-facebook-insights/.

---

[13] To access Facebook Audience Insights, your students will need a Facebook account.

[14] For the audience persona activities in this book, students are relying on one or a few data sources for educational purposes. The best way to build an accurate audience persona is to use multiple data sources. Research on social media and tools like Facebook Audience Insights can be combined with surveys, interviews, focus groups, as well as other data.

When narrowing down their search in Facebook Audience Insights, have your students consider geographic location and interests relevant to the target audience. This instructional video that I created for my students walks users through the use of Facebook Audience Insights:

- https://youtu.be/KDMTkR_8ozM

Learning Objective 3: Introduce Social Media Audits and Why They Are Performed
Learning Objective 4: Apply Social Media Listening Skills to Conduct Social Media Audit

What

The social media audit is an important tool for understanding how an organization is communicating online, what the online conversation about the organization looks like, and how the organization compares to its competitors online. In an article published in the Harvard Business Review, Professor Keith Quesenberry defines a social media audit as "a systematic examination of social data to help marketers discover, categorize, and evaluate all the social talk about a brand" (Quesenberry, 2015, ¶ 2). Freberg (2018) states that conducting a social media audit "is one of the most important things to do before implementing a strategic plan on social media" (p. 122).

Think of a social media audit as an assessment of past and ongoing social media efforts – which may include examining what social media platforms the organization is using, what the organization's online aesthetic is, what content the organization publishes and with what frequency, and what the nature of the organization's interactions are with fans and followers. A social media audit dives into the online conversation relevant to the organization. This assessment can go as far back in time as either deemed relevant to the situation (e.g., in the case that a crisis occurred and we want to know what is being said since the start of that crisis) or as far back as the tools being used to monitor the conversation will allow.

Show some examples of social media audits to your students. Talking through examples helps them understand what you are looking for and why. Dr. Tiffany Gallicano shares several wonderful examples of social media audits that were conducted by her students in 2015. While the social media landscape has changed since they were published, the methods behind the execution of these audits stand up to the passage of time:

- https://prpost.wordpress.com/2015/06/29/featured-content-from-my-j452-classes.

When possible, I like to show examples of work done by students – they don't have to be my students. Showing our students great work conducted by other students helps them see that quality work is attainable at their current level of experience.

Why

The social media audit is a completed, professional document that can be used in several ways. It is ground zero for the conversation your brand is going to lead. For example, a social media audit can show a client an organized and clear picture of the conversation around their brand. It can be used as evidence in support of some proposed action, such as a campaign.

Thinking about it from the campaign planning process perspective, a social media audit is a component of the conversation analysis. The conversation analysis, or communication audit, is an important component of background research on any client. It fits in Broom and Shaw's (2013) four-stage campaign planning process in stage one, defining the problem or opportunity, discussed in Chapter 2 of this book. As Freberg (2018) notes, such audits allow us "to evaluate what has been done, as well as the opportunities and challenges the organization or key personnel have failed to consider" (p. 122).

How can we change the conversation around a brand if we don't know what the conversation is? How can we accurately provide our primary audience with the information it needs to take the desired action we are seeking if we don't know what that public already thinks? We can infer what the primary audience thinks by seeing what they say. If we are taking on a new client, we cannot simply begin communicating without knowing what our client has communicated in the past. All of these points can be made in a brief lecture to your students.

But there is a different way to help bring this idea home to students and it can be accomplished in a five minute conversation. You have probably heard your students joking around about online 'creeping,' 'stalking,' 'scoping,' or 'Sherlocking' of friends or crushes. This is the common, generally harmless act of scoping out someone's online identity. We have probably all done it[15].

The other day, I was chatting with two students about building up their LinkedIn profiles as they prepared to graduate. One student said that she was 'totally stalking' her friend's LinkedIn profile because it was good and she wanted to set up her own profile in the same manner.

Ask your students how many of them have scoped out someone's online

---

[15] If this concept is new to you, then you may enjoy learning more about this phenomenon here: https://www.lifewire.com/what-does-creeping-mean-2655280 For the rest of us, don't worry – it is really common.

profile. You'll probably get some nervous giggles at first. Then, with a little coaxing, the conversation will open up. Ask students why they would 'creep' on another person's profile. You'll get answers such as 'to find out what they're up to,' 'to find out what kind of things they like,' 'to get to know them a little better,' and the like. Next, ask them how that information would be useful. You might get an answer such as, 'so I have some ideas of what to talk to them about,' or ,'to see if they are someone with whom I might have things in common.'

Here is an opportunity to help your students see the relevance of why they are doing what they are doing. From there, help them extrapolate to why a company would want to monitor this information. I do this by asking students to contemplate a silly scenario: "Let's say someone hired you to use your online creeping skills to really get the details on someone online. We'll call this person our target. Let's imagine you were an international spy or an FBI investigator. Probably, you would put together some kind of dossier about the target right? It would be very detailed with the target's profile photos, examples of posts the target has made, and perhaps what other people have said on the target's posts, or what people have said about the target on Twitter, or who appears to be the target's friends, et cetera, right?"

You will get some nods and some feedback. Ask the students what else would go into that dossier. Then ask them why that dossier would be valuable and who would use it. Depending on your students' imaginations, this conversation could go in several possible directions.

Then, tell the students, "Well, that's kind of what we are doing. It's like we have been hired to do some investigating. But, in this case, our target isn't a person. Our target is a brand. We want to know what the brand posts and what is being said about the brand." In other words, you can tell your students, a social media audit is "a dossier, or report, that results from systematic snooping around online to see what people are saying about our target and possibly what people are saying about our target's competitors." Lastly, ask your students why that might be a valuable thing to do and how a report like that could be used. Now that they have related the social media audit to something 1) that they have done – that is, online creeping - and 2) that gets their imagination going – high-level, top-secret sleuthing – they should have an easier time coming up with good reasons as to why the information gleaned from a social media audit could be valuable.

How

The social media audit assignment is in the chapter appendix. In addition, many free social media audit templates are available via a quick Google search[16]. You can also find templates in textbooks such as Quesenberry's

---

[16] For example, here are two:
https://sproutsocial.com/insights/social-media-audit/

Social Media Strategy: Marketing and Advertising in the Consumer Revolution (Quesenberry, 2018). Depending on what you want your students to learn, you can add or subtract from these templates. There is no one right way to conduct a social media audit. However, there are many common elements. Further, you will find that what your students can do will depend on what online tools you have access to. For example, if your class is running your department's social media, then you should have the login to their social media accounts and thus be able to get some analytics through tools such as Twitter Analytics and Facebook Insights. However, if your students are going to be looking at competitors as part of their social media audit, they will not have access to their competitors analytics.

Said another way, have your students use the tools available to them such as any free tools or industry software your class has access to. Industry tools are ideal but they are not required to complete this assignment. In reality, much of it can be done by searching social media platforms for information, such as conducting searches on https://search.twitter.com or browsing an organization's social media account on a given platform. Additional free tools that are nice but not necessary are provided in the social media audit assignment in the chapter appendix.

I require my students to conduct a social media audit of our department's social media and one similar department at a competing university. It is important that the competing department is of like comparison. I teach at a Council of Public Liberal Arts Colleges (COPLAC) university. Our communication department is small with, at the time of publication, four faculty members. We have a radio station, a television studio, computer labs, and the like. We offer certain classes and concentrations in our major. It would not make sense to have my students pick a communication department at a large, state university due to the many differences. I survey the class and help students determine if another department is indeed similar enough to ours. Another way to approach finding a competitor, is to ask your students what other universities they considered attending. One last challenge with having your students find a competing department is that the competing department must also have their own social media. Often, individual departments do not run their own social media. Thus, students may find a competitor and when they ask you to approve that competitor, lo and behold, they have found the university-wide social media and not the department's social media. This is because many department webpages will have social media icons on them that lead to the university's social media. It happens because many universities put links to their university social media on every page of their website.

I have broken down the social media audit assignment into two parts, with each part containing several sections (see the chapter appendix).

---

https://blog.hootsuite.com/social-media-audit-template/

Do

Students can begin working on the assignment in groups in class if your students have access to computers on day three of this unit (day five of the semester). Likely, it will take the remaining class time on day three after you provide the who, what and why, to find a like competitor to your university department. Day four of the unit (day six of the semester) is a lab day for them to work on their audit in class and for you to assist them.

Reflect

The reflection part of this unit is done once the students have completed and turned in their social media audit assignment. Thus, while it is part of Unit 2 on social media listening, it technically occurs on the first day of Unit 3 on the strategic brief. It serves as a great segue between the units.

Ask your students to take a few minutes to go through their completed social media audits. Ask them to evaluate our client and its competitor for things that were:

- A good fit for the brand.
- A bad fit for the brand.
- Creative, interesting, unexpected, or out of the ordinary.
- Not done very well or that could be improved upon.

Follow up with what, how, and why questions, such as how they would improve upon what was done, or how would they do it differently? What are some key things that they learned? Try not to get defensive when they critique your department's social media accounts, including the work you or students from past semesters have done. Soon, it will be these students' turn to strategize and create visually-stunning, audience-centric, engaging, discoverable content that will be published for the world to consume and critique. Remember, it will be your job to guide and lift these students up when they realize that running an organization's social media presence can be harder than it looks. That's next in Chapter 5 when we dive into Unit 3: The Strategic Brief.

Recommended Readings and More

Presentations

Burns, K.S. (n.d.). Social media analytics. Retrieved from https://www.canva.com/design/DADIUKfiayc/N3lHWoaekp8CFICzP2sL7Q/view.

Readings

Allen, T. (2016, January 11). How to create audience personas on a budget using Facebook Insights. *Moz.* Retrieved from https://moz.com/blog/facebook-insights-create-audience-personas-budget.

Balkhi, S. (2018, March 27). How to develop buyer personas using Facebook Insights. *Social Media Examiner.* Retrieved from https://www.socialmediaexaminer.com/how-to-develop-buyer-personas-using-facebook-insights/.

Basic Boolean operators explained. (n.d.). Boolean Black Belt-Sourcing/Recriting. Retrieved from http://booleanblackbelt.com/2008/12/basic-boolean-search-operators-and-query-modifiers-explained/.

Duncan, M. (2019, February 27). Teaching social listening in higher education. *Brain Waves Blog.* Retrieved from http://blog.campussonar.com/blog/teaching-social-listening-in-higher-education.

Fournier, S., Quelch, J., & Rietveld, B. (2016, August 17). To get more out of social media, think like an anthropologist. *Harvard Business Review.* Retrieved from https://hbr.org/2016/08/to-get-more-out-of-social-media-think-like-an-anthropologist.

Freberg, K. (2018). *Social Media for Strategic Communication.* Thousand Oaks, CA: Sage Publications, Inc.

Kim, C. M. (2016). *Social Media Campaigns: Strategies for Public Relations and Marketing.* New York, NY: Routledge.

Quesenberry, K.A. (2018, December 16). 337 tools and resources to improve your social media strategy for 2019. *Post Control Marketing.* Retrieved from http://www.postcontrolmarketing.com/337-tools-resources-improve-social-media-strategy-2019/.

Quesenberry, K. A. (2018). *Social media strategy: Marketing, advertising, and public relations in the consumer revolution.* (2nd ed.). Lanham, MD: Rowman & Littlefield.

Williams, H. (2018, May 4). Boolean query guide: Create relevant and accurate media monitoring searches. *Meltwater.* Retrieved from https://www.meltwater.com/uk/blog/boolean-media-monitoring/.

Sample Student Work

Gallicano, T. (2015, January 29). Featured content from my J452 classes. The PR Post. Retrieved from https://prpost.wordpress.com/2015/06/29/featured-content-from-my-j452-classes/.

Tools

Twitter Analytics (n.d.). *Twitter.* Retrieved from https://analytics.twitter.com/about.

Chapter 4 Appendix

Social Media Listening Exercise Activity Sheet

News Search
1. What top news posts and blog articles are discussing the brand? (Where were they published? Who was writing them?)

Social Media Search
2. Time and Date: When did the brand receive the most mentions on social media (Show a screen grab as evidence)? Can you find a reason? Hint: Try digging into social media posts or do a news search for that date about your brand.

3. Product Discussed: Which of the brand's products are popular on social media?
List them below:

4. What social media services (e.g., Instagram) are most popular when it comes to the brand? Least popular? Hint: Look at the volume of posts from each social platform.

5. Brand Sentiment: What % of posts about the brand are positive? What % are negative? (post a screen grab below).

6. How do people feel about our brand and its products? Hint: If you have a separate search for specific products, look at that sentiment score. You can click into the sentiment score to see specific posts that are scored positively, negatively, or neutral.

7. Try to find some examples of positive posts and negative posts (such as complaints about their products). Paste them below (either by copying the text or by doing a screen grab of an image).
Positive Posts

Negative Posts

8. Themes and Keywords: What are some themes you see in people's comments about the brand and its products?

9. Takeaways: What surprised you/what did you not know about how people feel about the brand that you now know from monitoring the social conversation about the brand?

The Audience Analysis Activity Sheet

Note to Students: Keep a soft copy of this – it can be used as the Main Audience persona for the Social Media Strategy Report (which will be assigned soon). Clean it up, remove unneeded text, and make it look professional.

Audience Persona	Demographics
(replace with photo of typical audience member – such as from a headshot in a social media profile you found in your research)	Name Age Gender Location

Backstory
Below, describe this person in detail. A little about them – What is their family situation? Education? Life experiences? How do they entertain themselves? What are their goals and aspirations? What are their primary motivations? What are their main worries in life?

About:
1. Given their backstory, why would they subscribe to your social media content? What is it that your client can bring to the table for this audience member?

2. What problem(s) can your client help this person solve via social media?

3. How does this person prefer to be communicated to / with? (Tone, voice, etc. For example, formal language? Down to earth? Explain)

4. What would be this person's ideal experience with your social media?

5. What do you, as members of this social media team, have in common with the target audience? What experiences do you share with them?

6. Describe the emotion this audience member will feel after consuming your content.

Evidence
Below, paste screen grabs that your team took while doing research using the tools I assigned that provide support for some of the claims you make above, specifically as it relates to your audience persona's demographics and backstory.

Facebook Audience Insights Persona Activity (Optional)

Create a Facebook Audience Insights specific persona for our client.

Go to audience insights: https://www.facebook.com/ads/creativehub. Log in with Facebook and then select 'audience insights' from the menu.
- Use Facebook Audience Insights to determine the following:
  - Demographics
  - Occupation
  - Education Level
  - Interests
  - Device Usage
  - Activity
- In an appendix, provide screen captures as evidence of your research. Tell the reader to see the appendix for screen grabs.

Example Facebook Audience Insights Research

The filter used in the 'interest' search option to conduct the Facebook Audience Analysis was: Baking. The potential target audience is for a subscription recipe and baking supplies service for persons interested in baking.

A recently-married 27-year-old woman named Sandra Smith. She is a university graduate from a mid-sized city in Tennessee. She works in health care. Her interests include family planning, healthy and earth-friendly products, cosmetics, and budget-conscious shopping.

Top match is bolded. Additional results are in parenthesis.
Demographics
- Gender: **Woman** (75% women, 25% men)
- Age: **27** (from 25-34 age range)
- Location: **Nashville, Tennessee**
- Relationship Status: **Married** (26% single, 21% relationship, 46% married)
- Education Level: **College** (22% high school, 69% college, 9% graduate school)

Household
- Occupation: **Health Care** (25% health care, 34% sales, 37% administrative services).
- Interests: Earth-friendly products and cosmetics, babies and children, reality television, fast fashion and budget-conscious shopping.

Device Usage

- **Uses mobile only** (0.3% desktop only, 33% both desktop and mobile, 67% mobile only)

Comments 21 times per month, clicks on 35 ads per month, likes 32 post per month and share 5 times per month.

The Social Media Audit Assignment

Overview
In teams, you will conduct a social media audit of our academic department AND a similar academic department at another university. Analyze at least 3 of our competitor's social media channels, ideally channels that are the same channels we use (e.g., Instagram, Twitter, Snapchat).

Useful Materials
- Social Media Audit Guide Questions (at bottom of this assignment).

Organization of Paper
1. Client Overview – 1-2 paragraphs describing who you're writing about.
2. Methods section – 1-2 paragraphs telling us what tools you used to complete your analysis (e.g., Facebook Audience insights, etc.)
3. Social Media Audit – Use the questions from Part 1 of the "Social media Audit Guide Questions" at the bottom of this document.
   a. Compare our academic department and a competing academic department.
4. Communication Audit - Use questions from Part 2 of the "Guide Questions" at the bottom of this document.
   a. Compare our academic department and a competing academic department.
5. Recommendations and Discussion
   a. Considering what you found, what conclusions can you draw about how our client could use social media? What recommendations do you have? How can we improve?
   b. Back up your claims by citing all references in text. Example: If you recommend the client posts 3 times per hour on Twitter, why? What is your source for this recommendation? – maybe it is discussed in lectures notes or a class text or assigned reading. Maybe your recommendation is based on things other universities are doing well. Maybe you need to do some external research.

Additional Requirements
1. Cover Page – Cover page with title of report and team member names.
2. Length – Body should be about 4-6 pages of text double-spaced (NOT including images, graphs, etc.).
3. Visuals – use screen captures of social media content, or create graphs or charts to communicate information such as numbers or comparisons.
4. Formatting – Use headers to organize your paper into sections.
5. Citations – All references to external material must be linked using embedded URLs.
6. Reference list - A list at the end of the document of any additional

readings or sources, including the URLs to their social media sites.
7.   Write paper as an essay – You can use bullet points for any lists.

Grading Criteria

▪   Writing quality should be professional.
▪   Organization, structure and flow of paper.
▪   Thoroughness of review and extent to which questions are addressed.
▪   Recommendations based on sound reasoning and evidence relying on credible external sources.
▪   Links to sources. Reference list.

Social media Audit Guide Questions

Part I. Organization's Social Media Overview

1.   Voice and Style
   ▪   It is important to note the style or tone the organization uses on their social media. This is conveyed through text in the posts, profile description, and other social content. It is also conveyed visually through color schemes, profile photos and graphics, images shared, etc.
   ▪   Is the organization consistent with how it portrays itself visually and textually across social platforms?
      o   Go to their social media account or blog and check it out.
      o   Look at the last dozen or two dozen posts.

2.   Social Media Publicity
▪   Look over their website/blog. Do they mention their social media presence? If so, how? Is a link present?
▪   Are they driving traffic between their website and social media sites? (e.g., do they link to their Facebook page on their website? Look over their Twitter posts – are they mentioning their Facebook?). In what ways? Are they driving traffic from their social media to their website? In what ways?

3.   Stats / Measurement
▪   *For our client:* Ask the professor for access to the class client's metrics, which can be obtained by logging you into the client's social media accounts such as Twitter and Instagram.
▪   *For our competitor:* Unfortunately we don't have access to our competitor's traffic stats. So rely on what you can get by looking at their account pages (how many likes for their Facebook page, followers on Instagram, Twitter, Pinterest, etc., and other similar stats can you find.)
▪   *For both our client and competitor:* These tools may add some extra insight:
      o   Twitter: Followerwonk.com (create free account with your Twitter.   click   analyze   followers) |

https://nexame.com/connect.php | https://socialblade.com | http://www.tweetstats.com/

- o Facebook – Go to:
    - https://www.facebook.com/business/insights/tools/audience-insights
    - And click 'go to audience insights.' Once logged in, select 'audience insights' from the menu on the upper left. Then, under 'interests' search the competitor.
- o Blogs – Focus on: Number of posts in a given time period (week / month), number of comments posts are getting, and any other stats that jump out at you.

Part 2. Conversation Analysis
Use the social search and listening tools I have provided to complete the below. I recommend creating a free account on Social Searcher (https://social-searcher.com). This is a key component of your social media audit. It is a look at the conversation going on around the brand.

1. What are they talking about?
   Look through some of their social media posts. What are the sorts of things this client seems to post about?
2. Who are they talking to?
   Who do they interact on social media?
3. Who talks about them?
   Search for their account username (ex: "@XYZdepartment") and identify top posters.
4. What is being said about them?
   Look at mentions of the brand and its social accounts. Identify examples that exemplify the conversation about them.
5. How often are they getting mentions in the past several months?
   Look at social media mentions across time to identify peaks. Can you find a reason for this?
6. Are the mentions positive / negative / neutral?
   Look at the sentiment score for the search you set up for them (ex: "Our university's name" "@XYZdepartment" etc.)
7. #Hashtags – Look at the hashtags identified on social-searcher.com. Or, search https://twitter.com/search and the search page on Instagram.com to determine any Hashtags associated with brand? Try a search with: https://ritetag.com/.

Matthew J. Kushin, Ph.D.

CHAPTER 5: UNIT 3. THE STRATEGIC BRIEF

The third unit orients students toward the strategic mindset they will take in planning and creating social media content for the class client. The goal is to have students create their social media strategy by developing a strategic brief. Also, students will start creating social media content.

Now that students have been introduced to the class and its main thrust, formed teams, and done some social listening, it is time to get into the fun stuff. That is, it is time for students to start working on their social media content strategy. They will do this by building a strategic brief which will be executed in the form of the strategic brief assignment.

Suggested Schedule: Weeks 4 and 5

1. Day 7: An Overview of Why People Share Content; Content Categories
2. Day 8: Time for Students to Brainstorm Content Categories; Introduce Content Calendars; Content Calendars Brainstorm
3. Day 9: Introduce Strategic Brief Assignment; Lab Day to Work on Strategic Brief Assignment
4. Day 10: Half of Class is a Lab Day and Half of Class Students Present Strategic Briefs

Unit Learning Objectives

1. Get students thinking critically about why users share content online.
2. Introduce students to what content categories are and help them brainstorm a few.
3. Introduce students to content calendars.
4. Teach students the skills for performing a strategic briefs.

The What, Why, How, Do, Reflect

Next, I will break down each learning objective above into its appropriate stages within the WWHDR framework. As before, you will note that we are dealing with a lesson unit, so some learning objectives do not contain each stage of the WWHDR framework because they build upon each other. For example, learning objective one can be covered in a brief 10 minute lecture as a segue to learning objective two.

Learning Objective 1: Introduce Reasons Why People Share Content

What and Why

Why do people share content online? Why do people click on links to articles that others share? These are big questions that both academia and industry have tried to answer. Indeed, online publications like BuzzFeed and Huffington Post have been built based on a keen understanding of what makes people share and click.

If they want to create content that will attract an audience, your students need a general understanding of why people share and click online content.

Start by asking students why they share the content they share. Ask them to think about some content they have recently shared or articles they recently clicked on. If you can spare a few minutes, have your students take out their phones and look at their social media feeds to find examples of content they recently engaged with. You'll get some great answers on what incentivizes your students.

Next, through a brief lecture, provide research and some anecdotes as to why some content gets shared and other content does not. Try to connect your students' answers with the research discussed below.

Before we discuss research, here is a brief anecdote. In September of 2018, I had an opportunity to visit the BuzzFeed offices in New York as part of a National Millennial Community trip. One of the employees offered this explanation as to what type of content works: "Things that make you feel less alone." That's a powerful idea. But let's break it down further.

Research on this subject goes back many years and an in-depth discussion is beyond the scope of this book. One of the earlier books I read on the subject was Dan Zarrella (2011) who wrote a book called *Zarella's Hierarchy of Contagiousness: The Science, Design, and Engineering of Contagious Ideas.* Perhaps most famously, Jonah Berger (2016) published *Contagious: Why Things Catch On.* This book was based, in part, on Berger's co-authored research on why people share content online.

Berger and colleague Katherine L. Milkman (2012), from the Wharton School of Business at the University of Pennsylvania, published an interesting study in the *Journal of Marketing Research* in which they explored three months' worth of *New York Times* articles to identify what types of articles were shared the most and why. The researchers examined each article to identify the emotions the article evoked. While articles which evoked positive emotions were shared more than negative ones on average, they found that negative emotions such as anxiety and anger increase sharing.

The authors thus identified that there are certain types of emotions that are high arousal, whether positive or negative, which compel sharing. For example, sadness is a low arousal emotion. Being sad turns us inward and thus does not encourage sharing. Awe-inspiring, anger and anxiety are high arousal emotions. These high arousal emotions compel sharing. The role of emotions in fostering online engagement has been confirmed in other studies such as Lui et al.'s (2017) exploration of the Facebook pages of Fortune 500 companies. Similarly, other research has shown that partisan content that elicits anger is more likely to be shared (Hassell & Weeks, 2016).

Okay, so emotions can trigger engagement with content. What else? Berger and Schwartz (2011) examine word of mouth discussion of products. They found that both immediate and ongoing word of mouth about products is influenced by two important factors: 1) The extent to which they are publicly visible and, 2) the extent to which they are triggered by the environment. For example, if a company mascot is a squirrel and that company has a funny commercial, when people see squirrels in their everyday life – say, climbing on a tree or jumping out in front of them while driving – they may think of the company. Extrapolate this idea into the social media space, and we could see that people may continue to chat online about content that they are triggered to think of. Thus, that funny squirrel video may get more traffic and more shares.

Building off of this and other research, Berger (2016) identified several factors that he argued contribute to the contagiousness of ideas. They are:

- Social Currency
- Triggers
- Emotion
- Public
- Practical Value
- Stories

For a detailed explanation of these concepts, I encourage you to watch the following YouTube video or read the following article. And since we are talking about sharing, feel free to share both with your students:

- https://youtu.be/HfSs_hOAkzY
- https://medium.com/the-nonfiction-zone/breakdown-of-contagious-why-things-catch-on-by-jonah-berger-a50e83a2f28a.

Although several years old, the research discussed above is about the psychology behind human behavior and thus the ideas persist across time. Research on the psychological motivations for word of mouth advertising goes back at least to 1966 (Dichter, 1966). You can watch a talk that Berger gave to Google on this subject here:

- https://youtu.be/FN4eDk1pq6U.

While Berger's book is surely not the end-all-be-all of why ideas spread, discussing it will provide your students with a foundational knowledge of why people share ideas. They can incorporate this foundational knowledge into their work.

Additionally, here is some interesting research worth sharing. A study published by Quesenberry and Coolsen (2018) in the *Journal of Current Issues & Research in Advertising*, examined the text of posts brands made to their Facebook pages to see which content increased likes, shares, comments, and ultimately organic reach. Because organic reach for Facebook page content has declined in the last few years, it is important to figure out what type of content users are likely to share because the Facebook algorithm is more likely to deliver content to us that our friends are engaging with. The researchers conducted a content analysis of the text from 1,000 Facebook brand posts to find out what increases engagement metrics that drive organic reach (i.e., likes, shares, comments). Specifically, they focused on 18 variables. This included aspects of posts such as photos and links, character and word length, number of hashtags, number of links, and number of brand mentions. They also looked at the content of the posts. Categories included new/now-style posts, posts focused on promotions or pricing, contests and sweepstake posts, corporate social responsibility (CSR) and social cause posts, events, celebrity-focused posts, questions, calls to action, posts that used exclamation points, fan contests and user-generated content, educational posts, and posts emphasizing specific times or dates (e.g., deadlines). Quesenberry and Coolsen found that Facebook brand posts that indicated something was new received higher shares and comments. Posts that emphasized a time or date, such as a deadline to complete an action, received higher shares. Educational posts, on the other hand, received fewer likes and comments. Interestingly, promotion posts, contest posts, and social cause or CSR posts were not associated with any of the three engagement metrics: Shares, likes and comments. One limitation to note of this study, is that it focuses on Facebook specifically. The authors note that content may perform differently on different platforms as different platforms offer different affordances.

If you would like to dig a little deeper, I suggest the following articles:

- https://www.nytco.com/press/results-to-the-new-york-times-customer-insight-groups-2013-the-year-of-video-survey/
- https://foundationinc.co/lab/psychology-sharing-content-online/
- http://www.pewinternet.org/2012/03/15/the-viral-kony-2012-video/
- http://www.journalism.org/2012/06/14/how-pop-tune-became-hottest-social-media-meme/
- http://www.postcontrolmarketing.com/research-engaging-facebook-brand-posts/

Learning Objective 2: Introduce Content Categories

What

Your students are probably excited to get working on creating social media content for the class client. Good. Leverage this excitement. But the students first need to learn a few tactics that will make their lives as newfound social media specialists a success. Imagine you told your students to come up with five creative ideas of things to do on your academic department's social media accounts. Once those five ideas are used up, the students would be back to the well to think of five more creative ideas. While creativity may be a bottomless well, the bucket of time has a hole in it.

So, you are going to teach your students to use content categories. Students only have to think of a few creative content categories. Then, they can build out content that will fit within those categories. Social media content categories are just that, categories of content types that individual pieces of content will fit within. Said another way, each category is a broad theme under which related social media content can be organized. Many pieces of social media content can be created that fit within a category. Therefore, the category can be repeated across weeks or months. Each category is just a content theme and within each theme your students will place similar content.

Image 3. Content 'Buckets' and Individual Social Media Pieces that Have Been Organized by Bucket

An effective way to explain this concept to students via a brief lecture is to use the term bucket in place of category or theme. Students are going to create several content buckets to organize their content into. Each piece of social media content they create must fit into one of the buckets. An illustration of this, such as shown in Image 3, can be used on a slide to drive this idea home. In this illustration, the pow, star, and lightning bolt symbolize individual pieces of social media content.

Once you have explained the concept, show some popular content categories that companies use when organizing their content. A quick Google search for "social media content categories" will show you many possible content categories. Below, I will share a few that I recommend. These have been inspired by myriad sources, including from authors like Michael Brito, Mark Schaefer, and sites like Social Media Examiner, as well as my own brainstorming.

1. Brand History – Content that relates to special moments in the brand's history, such as its birthday, release of important products, etc. Archival photos are great for this type of content.
2. Dates and Holidays – Pretty self-explanatory. Content that is created around well-known holidays like Independence Day.
3. Promotion – Content about your brand's products and business. Don't overdo it or your audience will tune out.
4. Helpful Hints and Tips – Tips to help your followers solve problems related to your brand. If your client is your academic department, then think of things like advice about registering for classes, studying tips, etc.
5. Audience Interests – Content aimed at relating your brand to the lifestyle and interests of your followers. These are things like references to popular culture, memes, and ongoings that help your followers see that you share common interests.
6. Behind-the-Scenes Stories – Content that highlights the real people behind your brand. That might be professors, academic advisors, et cetera that help your students get to know who you really are.
7. Human Stories – Stories of your customers and how your product has helped them or how they enjoy your product. For an academic department, that would be stories about your students or alumni and their achievements.
8. Web and Pop Culture Tie-ins – Content that leverages trends in popular and web culture such as movies, books and music. This is used simply as a way of saying, 'we get you.' There is an overlap here with the audience interests category.
9. Third Party Curated Content – Sharing content created by others.

A little research will help you find examples of brands using these type of content. For example, for the "Brand History Tie-Ins" category, I always love showing a post that Oreo did several years ago to celebrate its birthday. It shared a post of a nonagenarian grandmother who was born the same year Oreo was founded. The grandmother was eating an Oreo cookie. The post was a happy birthday wish to her. This post, therefore, also falls into the category of "Human Stories."

Next, let your students know that great content has one thing in common: It is story driven. Try to put storytelling at the core of the content that your students create. As the saying goes, people don't have time to listen to you talk but they have time to hear a great story. Brito (2013) talks about the concept of the content narrative in his book *Your Brand, The Next Media Company: How a Social Business Strategy Enables Better Content, Smarter Marketing, and Deeper Customer Relationships*. Content narrative is the use of storytelling to share what your brand stands for in a way that shows how your brand relates to its target audience.

Here's a simple example that brings together content categories and storytelling. Of the content buckets discussed on the previous page, let's take "Human Stories." How could your students create a "Human Stories" content bucket around seniors in your academic department? Perhaps something like a content bucket called "Senior Sum Ups" where short videos are created of seniors sharing their top highlights from the last four years. The videos could be short enough for Snapchat or Instagram and edited with fast jump cuts and text. By boxing the students into a short video length, they have to think creatively about how to extract this information from the seniors in their videos in a way that will work. Maybe each senior shares the top highlight of their year, or maybe they share the project they are most proud of, or maybe they share their favorite memory from their time in the department. What does this video series achieve? It tells the experiences and life of a student in your department from the mouths of the people who know what that experience is like the best, the seniors. Showing an example like this can help your students draw a connection between the concept of content categories, storytelling, and a workable idea.

Why

The Why here is a pretty easy sell. It is going to save the students time and energy. That way, they can focus the limited time they do have on creating awesome content. Second, this approach will add consistency to their social media, a consistency that their followers might not immediately recognize but that they will appreciate. Third, this approach will help teams stay on the same page because each member will know the content buckets they need to work within. Be transparent and tell your students this. It will only take a minute but will have a motivating factor.

How and Do

The How and Do sections happen sequentially via a brainstorming session. You want to show your students just how capable they are of applying what they have learned to come up with creative, engaging ideas. It can be challenging to get the creative juices flowing in class. Tips for helping your students start a brainstorming session can be found in the Brainstorming Drilldown section later in this chapter.

Let's get students brainstorming ideas for content categories. One way to do this is to get students doing a reflection on their social media audits.

Remember that at the end of the last chapter, I said that we would have students do the social media audit reflection on the first day of Unit 3. Have your students bring in their social media audit assignments. Give each team a few minutes to discuss the following questions among themselves. After a few minutes, jot some down on the board and host a class discussion.

What are some things the client and their competitor did that were:

- A good fit for the brand?
- A bad fit for the brand?
- Creative, interesting, unexpected, or out of the ordinary?
- Not done very well, uninspired, or that could be improved upon?

Now that students have some ideas of what appealed to them and what didn't, get them brainstorming about some possible content categories. Before letting your students loose to brainstorm, remind them that the content they are creating needs to match the voice and tone of your class client. So, if your client is all about being serious, then a funny series isn't going to work. Give the students ten minutes or so – they are probably bursting with ideas at this point.

Reflect

Upon ending the brainstorming session, ask teams to share a few ideas with the class. Encourage other teams to provide constructive feedback on the ideas. This will give teams a chance to pre-test their ideas and use this information to refine their ideas.

In examining ideas, raise questions around ethics to your class. While an idea may appear innocuous to the group, ask them to see how their ideas might be viewed by those not present or how multiple interpretations of an idea may arise. For example, in dealing with humor, remind students that misguided humor can harm. Conversations around the responsibility that comes with being entrusted with a client's reputation and credibility can help students see that words – or, in this case, posts - and actions matter.

Learning Objective 3: Introduce Content Calendars

Now that the ideas are flowing, it is time to teach students about organizing their ideas. As we will discuss in the next chapter when we start talking about the first content period, students will be creating content that will be published across several weeks. They will need to plan their content ahead of time and decide when that content will be published. It is time to introduce the social media content calendar.

What

A social media content calendar is just what it sounds like, a calendar for organizing social media content that will be published in a given time period for all relevant social media platforms. As Kim (2016) notes, a content calendar "helps develop purposeful interaction across all the platforms on which a brand is active" (p. 122). Usually, a content calendar contains the content plan for all the social media platforms a brand uses. But your students will only be planning content for the social media platform they are in charge of. The content calendar should also demonstrate how the planned content relates to campaign objectives (Kim, 2016). As a teaching tool, I like to have my students identify the content category for each post and how that post connects to the campaign's key messages.

There are many ways to organize a social media content calendar using social media calendar tools like Loomly.com, project management tools like Trello.com, or by simply programming content into social media dashboards like Hootsuite. You can also find free content calendar spreadsheets with a quick Google search of "social media content calendar template."

I have my students use a spreadsheet on Google Docs. I create the spreadsheet for the time period in which students will be creating content. Then, I have each team go onto that spreadsheet and enter their content so that all of the teams information is on one calendar. That way I can see it all in one place. Because I have my students create social media content for their social media audit assignment and for three content period assignments throughout the semester (as you will learn in later chapters), I create a total of four copies of the content calendar spreadsheets, each with the dates pre-programmed. They are:

- Social Media Audit Content Calendar
- Content Period 1 Content Calendar
- Content Period 2 Content Calendar
- Content Period 3 Content Calendar

In the chapter appendix you will find a link to a content calendar which you can use with your class. Note that this content calendar contains sheets for four weeks. To access the sheet for each week, click the tabs at the bottom of the spreadsheet. You will need to modify the spreadsheet for the time period for which your students will be creating content. For example, the social media audit assignment which I will discuss below requires the student teams to create content which will span across a two-week time period. Therefore, I delete two of the tabs.

Why

The social media content calendar saves time and helps student team stay organized. But you can also illustrate how it can help organize and execute content categories by developing weekly themes.

Tell your students to imagine they represent an imaginary chocolate bar brand, Mom's Chocolates Bars. Three content categories have been created for the brand's social media for next month: Human Stories, Helpful Hints and Tips, and Brand History. The students could organize these three categories by days of the week, thus creating weekly themes. For example, On Monday, posts using #MomsBarsMonday would highlight people who love Mom's Chocolate Bars. On Wednesdays, posts would highlight creative ways customers can use Mom's Chocolate Bars in recipes or perhaps decorations during the holidays. On Thursdays, photos of vintage Mom's Chocolate Bars collectibles and chocolates could be shared using a tie in to web culture via the #ThrowBackThursday or #TBT hashtags. Now that these three categories have been created, the team would just need to come up with content ideas for the month to fill out the content calendar.

Using an example such as this will help your students see how content categories and content calendars can be used in tandem as a time saving tool.

How

Show your students the content calendar that they will be using, such as the one I share in the chapter appendix, and explain to them how to use it.

Do

Using the above example of Mom's Chocolate Bars, have your students think about ways to take their content category ideas and merge them into weekly themes. For example, if they take the "Senior Sum Ups" idea from earlier this chapter, how could they create content around that each week? Simply put, they could do it each Friday and make it lighthearted and casual, the way Fridays are meant to be.

Reflect

As before, have your student teams share their ideas with the class to pre-test them and to get valuable feedback from the other groups on how they can tweak their content. As the student teams start to share ideas with each other, this is a great time to point out that collaboration between teams is encouraged. For example, if you have a team that is in charge of a blog and a team that is in charge of Instagram, they could work together to tease content that will be on the blog or to provide additional content that is not available in the blog post and which is only on Instagram. Here's an example. If the "Senior Sum Ups" were to take place as written blog posts (instead of videos as we discussed above), perhaps the Instagram team could drop a hint a few days before the post went live, teasing who the post might be about but not showing the person's name or face. Or, perhaps the blog post could mention that additional information, such as behind-the-scenes photos of the senior student who is being highlighted in the blog post, has been published on the Instagram feed.

Drilldown: Brainstorming

Getting the creative juices flowing in your class can be a challenge. Some groups of students will readily brainstorm with little prompting. But other students are more reserved. They may be shy. They may fear that others will not like their ideas and that they will be judged for having ideas that others see as unpopular or uncool. Try and remember what it felt like to be a student in an uncertain environment. As a professor, take it upon yourself to make brainstorming a nonjudgmental space. The less intimidating the environment seems, the more you may find your students willing to share.

One way to do this is to gamify brainstorming by setting up brainstorming prompts. Think of these prompts as brainstorming ice breakers. There are four components to a brainstorming session:

1. The ground rules
2. Who goes first, second, third, etc.
3. The ice breaking game
4. The brainstorming session

First, set the ground rules for your students. Some good ground rules are:

1. There are no bad ideas.
2. Have someone in your group write down all ideas shared.
3. Only speak when it is your turn.
4. When it is your turn, you have to share an idea.
5. Never criticize or say no to an idea shared.

Second, assign someone to go first and then have the students go around in a circle clockwise. This is a good idea because it is often hard to get the wheel turning because no one wants to go first. Here are a few ways that you can do that in a fun way that will get the conversation going:

- The person in your team whose birthday is closest to, or furthest from, today.
- The person in your team whose last name starts with a letter closest to the first letter of this month (example: If it is February, ask whose last name starts with F, E or G, D or H, and so on until you find the first person. If two people are equidistant from the first letter of the month, have them

flip a coin or start with the person whose first name comes first or last in the alphabet).

- The person in your team whose last name starts with a letter closest to first letter of the professor's last name, or the university's name, or the mascot of the sports team at the university, or the town the university is situated in.
- The oldest or youngest person in the group.
- The person with the most or least siblings.
- The person who has traveled to the most countries or states.
- The person with the most pets.
- The person whose hometown is furthest away.
- The person who has the most colors on their shirt.
- The person with the longest or shortest first or last name.

And, on, and on. You get the idea. Just don't let this part of the session take up too much time.

Third, it's time for the brainstorming icebreaker. There are many great brainstorming icebreaker games that will help get the creative juices flowing. I will share a few below. I hope that these games give you some ideas and prompt you to come up with your own brainstorming games. The point is that such icebreakers serve to remove barriers to 1) thinking of ideas, and 2) sharing those ideas. That's why we start brainstorming about something wacky or off topic. The more creatively you can get your students thinking at the start, the better off they will be when they need to start thinking of things related to your project. So in the icebreaker round, which should last no more than five minutes, start with a fun, off-topic prompt. Here are a few[17]:

- Show your students images of many different crayons or colored pencils and have them pick a color and come up with a goofy name for it.
- Have your students make up a silly name for a major league sports team in the town or city in which the university is situated. Have them decide what sport it is.
- Have your students invent a sport that is a mix of two existing sports and give it a silly name.
- Have your students rename your university's sports mascot.
- Have your students come up with a name for each member of their group using names similar to those found in a popular sci-fi, fantasy, or other epic novel or movie series.
- Have your students do a word association game where a student throws out a noun (say, 'cat') and each student has to think of a word that is related to a cat (e.g., cougar, lion, tiger, etc.). See how many times the students can go before they run out of ideas.

---

[17] Note that these prompts can also be used for ice breakers at the start of the semester once groups have formed teams as a way for students to get to know one another more quickly and in a fun, welcoming environment.

- Have your students come up with a band or musical group name for the team and give each person in the group an instrument to play and a fun stage name.
- Have your students come up with a new name for a movie or TV show that is popular, such as something that more accurately describes what the show is about. This can also be done for other things in popular culture such as songs. Just be careful here that the topics chosen are appropriate.
- Have your students write a haiku about their summer or winter break.
- Have your students come up with the name for a resort island they would like to live on and describe it.

As you can see, there are only as many silly brainstorming icebreakers as you can dream up.

Fourth, it is time to get teams brainstorming about the topic you want them brainstorming about, such as ideas for social media content categories. There are a few popular ways of running a brainstorming session. Here are two that I like:

1. **Round and round we go:** This is often called the carousel method. In short, the first person in the group provides an idea relevant to the brainstorming topic. Then, have a team go around in a circle. All members of the group must share an idea when it is their turn; there are no 'get out of jail free' cards or passes. By requiring each student to share an idea, you avoid group dominance by one or two people and 'shying out' by other people. No one else can speak unless it is their turn. Tell your students to go around the carousel two or three times.

2. **Yes, and:** "Yes, and" is a well-known rule of improv comedy. In short, improv comics are supposed to always say "yes, and," meaning that when one improv comic says something, the other improv comics never say no to it. They always add to it, taking the routine into sillier, and sillier places. Similarly, the "yes, and" can be used in brainstorming. In this brainstorming session, one person starts with an idea and the next person has to say "yes, and" and add to that idea. They cannot say no to an idea. They must either say "yes, and" or present a new idea. For example, if a student says "we should create content that highlights a class that students have to take each year while they progress through their degree in our department." Then another student might say something like, "yes, and we should do it by highlighting the final project in each class." The next student might say, "yes, and we should show how that final project will be useful as a resume builder or how it will otherwise be helpful when working as an intern or upon entering the workforce."

As you can see, brainstorming sessions do not have to be dreaded, dull affairs. Help your students get the creative juices flowing by bringing out the 'idea juicer,' that is, the brainstorming activities, and empower your students to start making some juice.

Learning Objective 4: The Strategic Brief

What

Inform your students that consumers and organizations use social media for different purposes. Uses and gratifications research has identified several reasons why consumers use social media. For example, Whiting and Williams (2013) found ten social media uses and gratifications, including social interaction, information seeking, to pass the time, for entertainment, for relaxation, for communicatory utility (that is, to foster communication), for convenience utility (that is, because it is convenient), to express opinions, to share information, and surveillance of others (e.g., "creeping," as discussed earlier). But the reasons students, and consumers more broadly, use social media are quite different than the reasons an organization uses social media. For organizations, social media exists as just one vehicle in the larger effort to achieve business goals.

Therefore, students need an understanding of the business purpose of the social media content plan they are going to create. While they've done some great brainstorming so far, it is here where you can help students see the need to focus their ideas on the class client's goals and objectives (Recall, that in Chapter 2, I went over setting up the background information for the project, which included establishing the client's goals and objectives).

The strategic brief, or creative brief, is where your students take their ideas and calibrate them to the client's needs, the situation, and the audience. If you have taught a strategic campaigns class, think of it as the components of the campaign plan boiled down to their most essential ingredients. The strategic brief is a summary of the strategic plan and the key information needed for the team and the client to be on the same page. In this way, it serves as a blueprint for the semester project. The format and contents of a strategic brief can take on different shapes. Just Google "creative brief template" and you will see what I'm talking about. But the goal is always to provide background information about the situation, explain what the project is trying to achieve, identify the target audience, discuss the proposed project, and cover its main considerations such as content, distribution plan and timeline. A strategic brief may also make note of competition.

Said another way, the background information that you sorted out in preparing this class, discussed in Chapter 2, contains much of the content that can be put into a strategic brief. But it will be the students' jobs to synthesize that information and look at it in the context of their role as aspiring social media professionals.

The strategic brief assignment is available in the chapter appendix. It is formatted to allow students to learn about what a strategic brief is while also answering questions that are pertinent to their learning in this class. Thus, the strategic brief assignment is partly a strategic brief and partly a professor's checklist to prompt your students to apply what they are learning.

The strategic brief is a team assignment. In summary, the strategic brief assignment requires the students to 1) provide an audience persona – if you recall from Chapter 4, the students have already created this and can plug it into their strategic brief assignments, 2) cover the goals and objectives for the campaign, 3) create a channel purpose statement – that is, a sentence or two articulating how the social media channel will be used and why (an example of which is in Chapter 2), 4) define the market differentiation for their social media, 5) identify the value the social media will bring to its consumers, 6) and create a proposed social media content plan based on the content categories the team decides upon (as discussed in Learning Objective 2 of this chapter). Lastly 7), the assignment requires teams to produce several publishable pieces of social media content for the social media channel they are responsible for. The goal is for you to be able to publish this content as the first content your students will have created for the class client.

This is a good time to review the background information that you have collected about the client.

Next, go over the assignment (see the chapter appendix). Note that the assignment includes a presentation portion. This is an important component of this class. As I discussed in Chapter 2, one of the checks and balances built into this class is the role students play in evaluating and providing feedback about each other's content. By having each team stand up and present its strategic brief to the other teams and to you, you are creating a platform for the other teams to provide feedback that will help you evaluate the proposed social media content. Have the teams evaluate one another by completing the strategic brief assignment presentation feedback form in the chapter appendix. Further, having your students present their briefs allows everyone in the class to know what the other teams are doing. This helps students feel more involved in the overall success of running the client's social media. Know that each time students create proposed social media content for the client, they will present it to the class. We will discuss how that works in upcoming chapters.

Why

Why should your students create a strategic brief? This begs a larger question: What is the business purpose of social media? Ask this question to your students. See what they say. They may say things like, 'to get more followers,' or 'for more people to know about your company.' These are a start and may be the right answer depending on the goals and objectives of the client. It is important, however, to emphasize to your students that ultimately, social media exists to drive revenue for your client. Everything else – more followers, more likes, more engagement – is ultimately secondary to revenue.

The question that needs to be answered is: What is the larger role that social media will play in the client's business goals?

For example, a company may want to boost its search engine optimization (SEO) ranking because it is using its landing pages to get leads. The company may want to create social media content around specific landing pages it has developed because social media content may impact search ranking[18].

The strategic brief helps the students couch their social media content strategy within the wider context and goals at hand.

If your class client is your academic department or university, there is another why question that needs some answering: Why should universities create social media content and how does that impact how students perceive the university? After all, your students are creating content for an academic department or university – which, let's be honest, might not be as exciting as creating content for a fashion brand, sports team, or technology company. In this case, share some information about how the social media content a university creates can shape student perceptions and attitudes towards that university. The following article, "How social media may influence student loyalty to a university," on the Journalists' Resources page of the Harvard Kennedy School's Shorenstein Center on Media, Politics and Public Policy contains a summary of a study on this topic and cites several related studies:

- https://journalistsresource.org/studies/society/education/social-media-university-student-brand-loyalty.

Feel free to do a little extra research on this.

How

Before your students begin the work of creating a strategic brief, provide a few social media case studies as assigned homework readings. You may also want to build in time in class to discuss these. I encourage you to find a few timely case studies to discuss[19]. For example, at the time I am writing this book, the Fyre Festival and social media influencer marketing is a hot case

---

[18] Some evidence suggests that social media can help SEO ranking (Ramdain & Taylor, 2018). While Google has publicly stated that social media does not have a direct effect on search engine optimization (SEO) efforts, others argue that it can play an ancillary role in driving search ranking by spreading content that then people find and link to creating more inbound links which can affect page rank (Traphagen, 2018).
[19] Find over 200 social media content marketing case studies here: https://www.simplemarketingnow.com/content-talks-business-blog/bid/134174/200-case-studies-social-media-and-content-marketing-examples#Libraries.

study topic. Discussing case studies can help students get at the business goals behind social media campaigns. In your discussion, help illuminate those and help the students see the connection between what the organization was trying to achieve and its content strategy.

Next, discuss your expectations for the social media content your students will be creating by going over your social media content guidelines and grading rubric (see the "What Makes For Good Content?" drilldown section in this chapter for a discussion of guidelines and grading rubrics).

Next, show your students a few tools that they can use to create their social content throughout the semester. If your students are versed in software such as Adobe Creative Cloud, then awesome! If not, don't worry. I've provided free, easy-to-use tools below. Recall that as part of the strategic brief, the students will be assigned to create social media content that your client can publish.

Social Media Image and Video Dimensions Resources
- Evergreen Social Media Image Dimensions Guide
    - https://sproutsocial.com/insights/social-media-image-sizes-guide/
- Evergreen Social Media Video Specs Guide
    - https://sproutsocial.com/insights/social-media-video-specs-guide/

Free Software for Making Social Media Graphics
- Canva (website and app) - https://www.canva.com/
- Stencil - https://getstencil.com/
- Sprout Social's list of 39 free tools for creating unique images - https://sproutsocial.com/insights/free-image-creation-tools/#design

Free Software for Making and/or Editing Video
- Adobe Spark (web and app) - https://spark.adobe.com/
- Kapwing (web) - https://www.kapwing.com/
- InShot (app): https://apps.apple.com/us/app/inshot-video-editor/id997362197
- iMovie (available on Apple computers)
- Movie Creator (Windows 10)

Free sources for Stock Photos
- Pexels - https://www.pexels.com/
- Pixabay - https://pixabay.com/

Social Media Ad Mockup Tools[20]

---

[20] While the software mockup tools in this list are for creating ads, they should be sufficient for providing the look and feel of a social media post for presentation purposes.

- Facebook, Instagram, Twitter, Pinterest - http://admocks.adparlor.com/
- Facebook Creative Hub - https://www.facebook.com/ads/creativehub

Do and Reflect

Set your students to work on the social media audit assignment (again, it's in the chapter appendix). Per Learning Objective 3 of this chapter, have your students use the content calendar in the chapter appendix to schedule out their content.

By giving students in-class lab time to get started on the project, you can assist the students and answer their questions. Engage with them. Ask them about their ideas and follow up with questions they can reflect on to improve their work before they turn it in. Try questions such as: 'I like this content category you have in mind and I'm interested in how you see this helping the client achieve their goals. Can you tell me more about that?' or 'What are some ways in which you see your social media content helping to differentiate our client from its competitors?' or 'How do you anticipate your target audience will respond to this post?' In dealing with ideas groups put forth that may raise ethical issues, point it out with questions like 'It's an interesting idea. Let's try to see it from multiple points of view. What are some ethical concerns our client (or, customers, or the public) might have about this?'

Drilldown: What Makes for Good Content?

As a professor, what are your expectations for high-quality content? Help your students meet those expectations by setting clear expectations. Content guidelines and grading rubrics can go a long way in clarifying those expectations. In creating content guidelines and a grading rubric, make sure your expectations are reasonable. Keep in mind that you are working with students who are learning how to do this. They are not experts.

Content guidelines help your students create content consistently to a high standard. Professor Anastacia Baird, a professor of communication studies at the University of La Verne, teaches an inspiring undergraduate social media class. She has developed excellent content guidelines for her students as well as an excellent rubric for grading her students' social media content. In the chapter appendix, you will find content guidelines that I provide to my social media students. Those guidelines are inspired by and based largely on the content guidelines that Professor Baird has created and shares with her students. The guidelines provided in the chapter appendix are tweaked slightly from Professor Baird's original guidelines for the purposes of fitting the context of my class.

I have also provided Professor Baird's grading rubric in the chapter appendix. The rubric I use in my classes is based largely on Professor Baird's rubric.

Recommended Readings and More

Readings

Allen, M. (2016, October 24). Breakdown of "Contagious: Why things catch on" by Jonah Berger. *The Nonfiction Zone*. Retrieved from https://medium.com/the-nonfiction-zone/breakdown-of-contagious-why-things-catch-on-by-jonah-berger-a50e83a2f28a

Berger, J. (2016). *Contagious: Why Things Catch On*. New York, NY: Simon & Shuster.

Brito, M. (2013). *Your brand, The Next Media Company: How a Social Business Strategy Enables Better Content, Smarter Marketing, and Deeper Customer Relationships*. Indianapolis, IN: Que.

Clayton, B. & Ordway, D.M. (n.d.). How social media may influence student loyalty to a university. *Harvard Kennedy School Shorenstein Center on Media, Politics and Public Policy Journalist's Resource*. Retrieved from https://journalistsresource.org/studies/society/education/social-media-university-student-brand-loyalty/

Hitlin, P., & Tan, S. (2012, June 14). How a pop tune became the hottest social media meme. *Pew Research Center*. Retrieved from https://www.journalism.org/2012/06/14/how-pop-tune-became-hottest-social-media-meme/

Raine, L., Hitlin, P., Jurkowitz, M., Dimock, M., & Neidorf, S. (2012, March 15). The viral Kony 2012 video. *Pew Research Center*. Retrieved from https://www.pewinternet.org/2012/03/15/the-viral-kony-2012-video/

Results of the New York Times Customer Insight Group's 2013: The year of video survey. (2013, October 17). *The New York Times Company*. Retrieved from https://www.nytco.com/press/results-to-the-new-york-times-customer-insight-groups-2013-the-year-of-video-survey/

Schaefer, M. (2015). *The Content Code: Six Essential Strategies to Ignite Your Content, Your Marketing, and Your Business*.

The psychology of content sharing online in 2018 [research]. (2018, December 19). *Foundation*. Retrieved from https://foundationinc.co/lab/psychology-sharing-content-online/

Quesenberry, K.A. (2019, February 27). What makes Facebook brand posts

engaging? [research]. *Post Control Marketing*. Retrieved from
http://www.postcontrolmarketing.com/research-engaging-facebook-brand-posts/

Videos

FightMediocrity (2015, August 13). Contagious: Why things catch on by
Jonah Berger | Animated Review. Retrieved from
https://www.youtube.com/watch?v=HfSs_hOAkzY&feature=youtu.be

Talks at Google. (2013, March 27). Jonah Berger: "Contagious: Why things
catch on" | *Talks at Google*. Retrieved from
https://www.youtube.com/watch?v=FN4eDk1pq6U&feature=youtu.be

Chapter 5 Appendix

Social Media Content Calendar Template

Note to the reader: Access the social media content calendar template via the URL below. You can download the calendar for your own use or save a copy to your Google Drive folder. To save it to your Google Drive, sign into Google. Then, click "File" -> "Make a Copy" and follow the instructions. I encourage you to make a second copy and use that copy to share with your students. That way, you'll have the original copy just in case. You can make the file shareable to your student teams by clicking the "Share" button in the upper right hand corner of the spreadsheet. Choose the option to let anyone with the link edit the file. This will allow your class to all go to this file and edit it. Simply share the URL that Google generates with your students.

By letting all of your students edit the same file, you can assign each team to add their content to the same content calendar. Thus, you can easily see all of the proposed content on one content calendar spreadsheet.

Be sure to modify the dates on the calendar to fit the assigned time periods that you want your students creating content for.

Full URL:

https://docs.google.com/spreadsheets/d/1F-MT3bhOa0OLPMtyevfDI5ubcN8muE9n-yUCT1eRGb4/

Short Link (case sensitive):

http://bit.ly/31ndfQc

Strategic Brief Assignment

Note to the reader: In Part 3 below, you will want to modify the time period for which you want the students creating proposed content based on your needs. I have my students create content that will be published over the course of a two-week period starting the week after the assignment is due. During those two weeks, I am assigning and covering Content Period 1, which I will discuss in the next chapter. I will go over the timetable for scheduling content in more detail in the next chapter. Also, in Part 3 below, the instructions tell the students to organize their content using the content calendar the professor will provide. This is a reference to the Social Media Content Calendar Template in this chapter Appendix on the previous page.

Purpose
Create 1) background of your plan, 2) your social media plan and its rationale, and 3) create publishable content.

Paper
Part 1 Strategic Brief
Cover Page
1. Audience Persona – Complete one audience persona for the primary audiences that we identified for this class.
2. Goals and Objectives – list any goals and objectives provided by the professor. If none were provided, create them.

Channel Purpose, Differentiation, and Value
1. Social Media Channel Purpose Statement: Write a statement articulating how the social media channel your team is responsible for will be used and why.
2. Differentiation: How do you differentiate our client from the competition? How will you use social media to help our client stand out from its competitors?
3. Value: What value will your content bring to your consumers? Examples may include how to's, entertainment, news and updates, etc.

Team Assignments and Workflow
1. Complete and insert the "Roles and Responsibilities" listed below. Determine each person's position. If there are others your team needs, add and explain them.
2. Complete the "workflow" below. Insert it.

Part 2: Content Plan
1. Content Proposal – Your general plan for the semester for the content you want to create and your reasoning for it. These can be a sentence or two long.
2. What is the conversation you want to lead?
3. What is your content plan for leading that conversation? (that is, what are you planning to create)

4. What does success look like for your plan?
5. Fit with Goals and Objectives – explain how your plan fits with the goals and objectives you listed in Part 1 above.
6. Audience – explain why your content will resonate with primary and secondary audiences.
7. Campaign theme – explain how your proposed plan fits within the campaign theme the professor provided.
8. Fit with readings / research – Explain how your plan fits with SPECIFIC examples from assigned readings. Use additional research you've done (readings; via use of social media tools in class activities).

Part 3: Content We Can Publish
Note: This is not what you recommend / or a pilot of what you will create. It is completed content to be published.
1. Publishable Samples – these are in the form of the Team's editorial calendar spread over 1-2 weeks, as you decide necessary. <u>I plan to publish these.</u>
   a. Organize your content using the content calendar template I have provided.
   b. Requirements:
      i. Twitter / Instagram / Snapchat / Facebook: 2 samples of publishable quality.
      ii. Blog: 1 blog post
         1. For each blog post you need to provide 2 different tweets to promote in your content calendar.

Expectations:
- Appropriateness of work to the situation, audience, and client.
- Professional writing and organization expected.
- Length: As needed to complete above sections thoroughly.
- Thorough completion of each section of each part of the paper.

Presentation
Your group will present your proposal, content plan, and samples to the class. You need to organize your material and determine the most important information to convey. You can't cover the entire proposal in depth in 10 minutes. Focus most of your time on Part 2 of your proposal document.

Q&A / Evaluation
Afterwards, your classmates (who are roleplaying as the client) will evaluate your presentation and will be encouraged to ask you questions.

Expectations
- Do not treat this as a presentation for a class. Treat it as a presentation at your job.
- Business casual.
- Polished, practiced, professional presentation style.

- Time: about 10 minutes
- Visuals – e.g., slides or other visuals.

Grading Criteria

- Dress: Credit taken off for unprofessional dress.
- Presentations more than two minutes outside of the time window will receive a grade deduction.
- Thoroughness of coverage of the sections of your proposal.
- Professional, organized, and practiced presentation. Deductions for signs that teammates are not on the same page or uncertain of their role in presentation, who talks when, etc.
- Professional and appropriate integration of visuals to bolster presentation.
- Persons late to their team's presentation will receive 10% off their total grade for the assignment.

Roles and Responsibilities

Teams succeed when members have clear roles and responsibilities. Team members can be assigned to multiple roles; multiple people can be assigned to one role.

Assigned Team Member	Role
	Team Lead – person responsible for turning in work, and overseeing general project.
	Monitor - Person monitoring social web; ongoings in community and around campus; trends, pop culture.
	Head Writer - Person(s) with stellar writing and editing skills. Responsible for drafting content, or editing content drafted by others.
	Multimedia – Person(s) with strong photography/videography, editing, or other related skills. Responsible for creating multimedia content; or editing / helping others who are creating content.
	Amplifier – Socially connected person who can build support: Spread word online and offline; Recruit brand ambassadors
	Others - Explain

Work Flow

This is the planned process of completing tasks.

- Step 1:

- Step 2:

- Step 3:

- Step 4

- Add steps as needed.

Example:
- Step 1: We will all meet to brainstorm and come up with topics.

- Step 2: Each person will be assigned specific tasks to complete by a given date.

- Step 3: We will all meet at 4 p.m. on Fridays since everyone is available, and go over everyone's work.
-
  Step 4: Jan and Miguel will go over what was shared to ensure the text is great, and the photos are formatted to be uploaded to Instagram. Everyone else will practice the presentation, and present it.

- Step 5: Vishal will upload the files on the due date.

Strategic Brief Assignment Presentation Feedback Form

Instructions:
Rank each on a scale of 1-7, where 1 means "strongly disagree" and 7 means "strongly agree." Look at the overall presentation as a whole, as opposed to individual students.

Question	Score:
Plan Overview	
I could easily understand what their plan was.	_____
If I saw this content being published by our client, I'd be proud to say I helped create it.	_____
The plan was creative and unique - I could tell they put some serious thought into it.	_____
Goals and Objectives	
Their plan fit with the goals and objectives and were in line with the background research the professor provided about the client.	_____
Audience	
Excellent job considering the needs, wants, desires of the audience and creating content that audience would find compelling.	_____
Themes	
Content fit very well into our campaign's theme.	_____
Content fit very well into the content categories	_____
Channel Purpose	
Their channel purpose was clear.	_____
Their content and their plan fit very well with their channel purpose.	_____
Readings and Outside Research	
They clearly considered content from OUTSIDE class lecture in their plan.	_____
The rationale they gave for readings/research OUTSIDE of class was sound, and provided reasoning and logic for the decisions they made.	_____

Content Examples: Evaluate the content examples they proposed publishing in terms of professional quality: (Writing, visual, editing, etc.), match to goals, objectives, etc., other considerations you find important.

Which of their examples (if any) do you:

Suggest we publish: Suggest we don't publish

Social Media Grading Rubric

Lab Shift Post Rubric | Baird | Fall 2018	Proficient	Progressing	Emerging	Below Expectation
Name:		**Editor:**		**Grade:**
Style/Tone	Uses the appropriate voice/tone for target audiences (Hint: We target current and prospective students on IG, alumni on Facebook, and the university as well as the greater communications community on Twitter). Content was appropriate for the audience and includes a clear CTA if relevant (encourages engagement through the text).	Uses the appropriate voice/tone for target audiences (Hint: We target current and prospective students on IG, alumni on Facebook, and the university as well as the greater communications community on Twitter). Content was appropriate for the audience.	Voice/tone is not appropriate for target audience (per platform) and/or content was **not** appropriate for the audience.	Voice/tone is not appropriate for target audience (per platform) and/or content was **not** appropriate for the audience.
	Consistently follows AP Style.	Misses some AP Style rules.	Misses some AP Style rules.	And/or does not follow AP Style.
Grammar, Punctuation, Spelling	Uses appropriate grammar that helps readers understand meaning. No errors in punctuation. All words spelled correctly, including names, titles and @usernames.	Uses appropriate grammar. No errors in punctuation. All words spelled correctly, including names, titles and @usernames.	Uses appropriate grammar that helps readers understand meaning. Some errors in punctuation. Some words are spelled incorrectly, **not** including names, titles and @usernames.	Does not use appropriate grammar. Some errors in punctuation. Some words spelled incorrectly, including names, titles and @usernames.
Optimizing by platform to increase REACH	Uses geo-location tags when appropriate. Uses appropriate hashtags for IG	Uses geo-location tags when appropriate. Uses appropriate hashtags for	Uses some appropriate hashtags for IG and Twitter including	Does **not** include the appropriate standard hashtags #ulaverne and

Credit: Professor Anastacia Baird, assistant professor of public relations in the in the College of Arts and Sciences at University of La Verne.

and Twitter including #ulaverne and #ulvcomms for all posts. #ulvsocial for posts directly related to the class. #knowyourleos and #leofamily for alumni and current student posts. #leoforlife for alumni posts. Also includes relevant trending or relevant hashtags that relate to the post and to our target audiences.	IG and Twitter including #ulaverne and #ulvcomms for all posts. #ulvsocial for posts directly related to the class. #knowyourleos and #leofamily for alumni and current student posts. #leoforlife for alumni posts.	#ulvcomms for all posts. #ulvsocial for posts directly related to the class. #knowyourleos and #leofamily for alumni and current student posts. #leoforlife for alumni posts.	#ulvcomms for all posts. #ulvsocial for posts directly related to the class. #knowyourleos and #leofamily for alumni and current student posts. #leoforlife for alumni posts.
Optimizing by platform to increase ENGAGEMENT Uses platform-specific engagement tools or techniques to encourage audience engagement. (E.g. polls). Includes @usernames when appropriate. Includes a CTA when appropriate for the post.	Uses platform-specific engagement tools or techniques to encourage audience engagement. (E.g. polls). Includes @usernames when appropriate.	Uses platform-specific engagement tools or techniques to encourage audience engagement. (E.g. polls).	Does not use engagement tools or techniques to encourage audience engagement.
Visuals All visuals were appropriate for the content. Visuals were high quality in terms of technique (lighting, focus, framing, composition), and original content created by the producer. Visuals were interesting and	All visuals were appropriate for the content. Visuals were high quality in terms of technique (lighting, focus, framing, composition), and original content created by the producer. Photos for profile posts are	Visuals were **not** high quality in terms of technique (lighting, focus, framing, composition) and not designed to grab attention. Photos for profile posts lack context to help tell a story about who they are and what	Visuals were **not** high quality in terms of technique (lighting, focus, framing, composition), and/or were **not** original content created by the producer and did not include photo credit.

Credit: Professor Anastacia Baird, assistant professor in the in the College of Arts and Sciences at University of La Verne.

eye-catching. Visuals and text work together to tell a story. Visuals are well composed and designed to grab attention. Photos for profile posts are interesting and help tell a story about who they are and what they're about.

interesting and help tell a story about who they are and what they're about.

they're about. If photo was not original proper photo credit was given i in the format of Photographer First Name Last Name @username.

Credit: Professor Anastacia Baird, assistant professor in the in the College of Arts and Sciences at University of La Verne.

Social Media Brand Guidelines

Please follow these guidelines to conform to our client's branding.
You will be graded against these guidelines in the assignment rubric.

<u>Content Guidelines</u>

1. **Hashtags:** Use relevant hashtags. Search a hashtag on the social media platform before recommending it to ensure it is brand appropriate. Department hashtags are: _____, University hashtags are _____
2. **Class Names:** When talking about a class, use the full name of the class and course
   - number in this format: COMM #: Name Spelled Out
   - Example: COMM 322: Social Media
3. **Proper Titles and Names:** Spell check the name of all persons and entities mentioned. When talking about a person, use their proper title such as Dr. Smith, President Jones.
   - Per AP guidelines:
     o Capitalize a title when it comes before a person's name. Lowercase a title if it's used after a name.
     o When talking about a company or organization, including our university, Twitter, Snapchat, etc. use the full, proper name and capitalize the name.
4. **Tag to help others find your content:** Find and tag the social media handle of all persons or entities mentioned in a post.
   - Example: Great job @Personssuchandsuch on your new internship with @ImportantCompany!
5. **Engage your audience:** Consider how your content can get engagement from your audience.
   - Ask questions and encourage comments.
   - When creating content with links, tease the audience with mystery so that they will want to click the link.
     o Example: What's next for @Awesomestudent after graduation? Find out in our latest installment of OurDepartment Grad Life
     o Use brand-appropriate, relevant cultural references - memes, songs, shows, etc.
6. **Be on Message:** Ensure your content is appropriate to our semester project's audience, goals and themes.
   - Use a friendly but professional tone and style.
   - Share your idea with someone else and ask for their feedback.
7. **Language:** Just because you're writing for social media, doesn't mean grammar, punctuation and spelling go out the window.
   - Run your content through a spell-checker.
   - Have a friend copy edit your text.

- Don't forget apostrophes - be sure to add possessives where necessary.
  - Example: "A big congrats to Jerome Smith for being OurUniversity's first student to win the XYZ scholarship."

Credit: This is a slightly modified version of Professor Anastacia Baird's social media branding rubric. Anastacia Baird is an assistant professor in the College of Arts and Sciences at University of La Verne.

CHAPTER 6: UNIT 4. CONTENT PERIOD 1, SOCIAL MEDIA INFLUENCERS, AND CONTENT CREATION BEST PRACTICES

The fourth unit of the semester brings together the work students have done so far. Students begin creating the social media content for the client. The unit goal is to have students complete the Content Period 1 assignment. In this unit, students will execute the plans from their strategic briefs and pitch their content to the class.

We are now entering the part of the semester that is dedicated to the creation of social media content for your class client. Students will be planning and creating social media content based on the plan they outlined in their strategic brief. They will pitch their content to the class via presentations. Once that content is turned into you, you will grade it and make the ultimate decision as to what content gets published. Then, you will plan to have it published.

There are three content periods. Each period aims to cover a pre-determined set of time in the semester. This way, students are getting the assignment weeks in advance, working on creating the content, and then turning it in to you so that you can grade it and get it published. It works in the below phases:

1. Assign: Content period is assigned.
2. Create: Students work on content period and are learning new class material.
3. Present: Content is turned in to professor and pitched to class.
4. Grade: Content is graded.
5. Publish: Content is being published during the pre-determined set of time. Meanwhile, students have been assigned the next content time period and are working on the social media content for that next content period.

If you have followed the schedule outlined in the previous chapters, you should now be entering the sixth week of the semester. If you followed the plan in Chapter 5, your students turned in their strategic briefs by the end of the second day of classes in week 5. As part of that assignment (see The Strategic Brief assignment in the Chapter 5 Appendix), students were required to create social media content for the class client that could be published over the following two weeks.

Therefore, you now have content to publish to your client's social media for the next two weeks – weeks 6 and 7. Thus, during weeks 6 and 7, students will be assigned Content Period 1 and will be working on it (We will discuss Content Period 1 in this chapter). At the end of those two weeks, the students will present to you their content plans. After that, outside of class time, you will be publishing their Content Period 1 content over the three weeks that follow – weeks 8, 9 and 10. During week 8, you will assign Content Period 2, which will be discussed in Chapter 7.

The below tables show proposed schedules for the weeks of the semester during which students will be working on an assignment and the weeks during which the content from that assignment will be published.

The tables include the strategic brief assignment discussed in the previous chapter. The first table is for a fall semester and the second table is for a spring semester. For purposes of clarity and simplicity, this book is written to follow the fall semester and the syllabus included in this book is based on a fall semester. With minor modifications, you can adjust the assignments to work with a spring semester as shown in the second table. So as to be consistent in the requirement for students to create content for three weeks during Content Period 1, students are not required to create content for spring break.

These schedules both assume a 15-week semester (including a week off for those universities with a week-long Thanksgiving or spring break). Note that for Content Period 3, the social media content your students will create will be published after the semester is over. This works particularly well for keeping content going during winter breaks between semesters or in the time leading up to and after graduation in the spring.

Fall Semester

Assignment	Weeks to Work on in Class	Weeks Content will be Published
Strategic Brief	Weeks 4 and 5	Weeks 6 and 7
Content Period 1	Weeks 6 and 7	Weeks 8, 9 and 10
Content Period 2	Weeks 8, 9 and 10	Weeks 11, 12, 13, 14, 15
Content Period 3	Weeks 11, 12, 13*, 14, 15 *Thanksgiving break	Five weeks including finals week and four weeks after the semester ends.

Spring Semester

Assignment	Weeks to Work on in Class	Weeks Content will be Published
Strategic Brief	Weeks 4 and 5	Weeks 6 and 7
Content Period 1	Weeks 6 and 7	Weeks 8, 9 and 11 (with a week off for spring break)
Content Period 2	Weeks 8, 9, 10* and 11 *Spring break	Weeks 12, 13, 14, 15
Content Period 3	Weeks 12, 13, 14, 15	Five weeks including finals week and four weeks after the semester ends.

Publishing content for several groups across several platforms can be a lot of work. But it is not something you need to spend your time doing if you can make other arrangements. Offload the task of publishing the graded content. You can do this by requiring your own students to publish the content, by using graduate assistants or teaching assistants, or through other means. I use a group of students who have already completed the class to help me publish the content. The group usually consists of two to four students. We meet briefly every time I am done grading a content period. These former students do not see any grades nor any of the feedback I provided to the students enrolled in the class. They are not made aware of any content that I do not plan to publish. They only get the content that I want them to publish and a content calendar to follow for doing so.

If you have set up everything well in the strategic brief assignment as it was outlined in the previous chapter, then you have already done a lot of the legwork to set your students up for success in content periods 1, 2, and 3. The heavy lifting is done. The bulk of the work now comprises three components:

1. Teaching additional knowledge – During each content period there will be new knowledge that students will learn and, in many cases, incorporate into that content period. You can adjust the learning focus of these content periods to teach within them whatever content you feel is most important for students to be learning as the social media field evolves. In this book, we will focus on teaching about influencers in Content Period 1, teaching about social media metrics and ongoing social listening in Content Period 2, and discussing paid social media in Content Period 3. But you may want to bring in guest speakers, discuss social media policies, dive into more case studies, explore personal branding, drill down on specific social media platforms, or cover other content pertinent to your department's learning goals for the course.

2. Coaching students in executing their plans – Students created a vision in

their strategic brief. Now, they need to execute that vision. From my experience, students sometimes have a hard time staying focused on the plans they put forth. New ideas will pop up or they simply won't know how to take the idea in their strategy and realize it through the creation of content. Utilize lab time and meetings with teams to talk things over as students begin working on content. You may go to meet with a team and the team suddenly says, "We're going to create a video of a cat and a dog wearing our university's gear." "That's a fun idea," you say. After all, it's cute and visual. "But, what does it have to do with your original strategy?" Coach them. Pull them back toward their strategy. Guide them to success.
3. Helping students develop skills – Lab time is not a waste of learning time. Lab time is where a lot of learning happens. Give students the tools and software, such as those discussed in above chapters, and let them develop and hone their social media and digital storytelling skills.

Suggested Schedule: Weeks 6 and 7

1. Day 11: Assignment Overview and Introduction to Influencers
2. Day 12: Digital Influencers and Lab Time to Work on Content Period 1 and Finding Influencers
3. Day 13: Content Period 1 Lab Day (Optional: Social Media Content Creation Best Practices)
4. Day 14: Student Presentations

Unit Learning Objectives

1. Introduce students to the history and development of the concept of influencers and help them develop the creative and problem solving abilities to identify digital influencers.

Content Period 1 Assignment

The Content Period 1 Assignment is available in the chapter appendix. Go over the assignment with your students.

Recall that the teams will be required to present their content to the class. There is a presentation evaluation sheet in the chapter appendix which you can have your students complete. This form is a great starting point for creating a dialog for constructive peer feedback after each team presents. Collect these completed evaluation forms to assist you in evaluating each team's work.

The What, Why, How, Do, Reflect

Learning Objective 1: Introducing Influencers

What

These days, the term 'digital influencer,' 'social media influencer,' or just 'influencer' probably needs little introduction for your students. They likely know more influencers in their interest niche than you do. Just ask them.

The power and peril of influencer marketing has been getting a lot of attention recently. This is most famously due to documentaries like *Fyre: The Greatest Party that Never Happened* on Netflix and *Fyre Fraud* on Hulu about the disastrous failure of the Fyre Festival. The Fyre Festival promoters made extravagant promises about the event on social media. They leveraged several famous social media influencers to make these promises. When the festival collapsed in failure and attendees did not get what they were promised, it raised questions about the legal and moral responsibilities social media influencers have in making endorsements.

Beyond the headlines, though, influencers have been making a splash for years. In fact, the concept of influencers in the communication theory literature dates back at least to Paul Lazarsfeld, Bernard Berelson and Hazel Gaudet's 1948 book, *The People's Choice: How the Voter Makes Up His Mind in a Presidential Election*. It can also be traced back to the follow up research of Elihu Katz and Paul Lazsarsfeld in the 1940s, which was published in 1955 in their book *Personal Influence: The Part Played by People in the Flow of Mass Communication*. So let's start your students there with a brief lecture. Yes, I'm taking you back to communication theory class from the 'old days' when we professors were in school. I'm talking about the two-step flow of communication which later developed into the multi-step flow of communication and which set the groundwork for diffusion of innovations.

Here's a quick rundown of the two-step flow of communication that you can use as the foundation for a brief lecture to your class. The following paragraphs about the two-step flow of communication are cited from a classic textbooks from back when I was a graduate student, *Milestones in Mass Communication Research: Media Effects* by Lowery and DeFluer. The two-step flow of communication is built on the notion that primary groups – one's direct social relations – have a significant impact on behavior. These primary groups impact all aspects of our lives. They help us make meaning of the world around us and that meaning becomes our reality. Research began to show that information flows from the media through these groups (Lower & DeFluer, 1995).

Another important notion is that there are certain individuals within our primary groups who are opinion leaders. These are people that we turn to for advice about beliefs, purchases, likes, dislikes, and much more. Often, the transaction between opinion leader and follower is one that occurs without either party being aware of it. So while we get information from the media, a lot of our information and influence comes directly from others (Lowery & DeFluer, 1995).

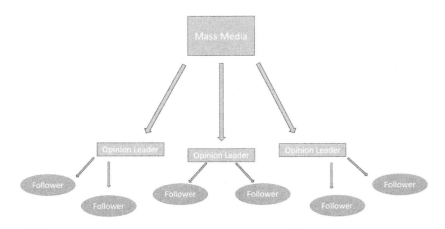

Image 4. The two-step flow of communication shows information flowing from mass media to opinion leaders and from opinion leaders to opinion followers.

The Erie County, Ohio 1940 election study is the first to uncover the idea of the opinion leader, giving us the model of the two-step flow of communication. Here's how it worked: When it came to decision-making in an election, Lazarsfeld and colleagues found that information passed from the mass media (e.g., newspapers and radio) to opinion leaders, then from opinion leaders to opinion followers. Within that flow, the opinion leaders imbued the information with their own opinions and interpretations. Opinion leaders tended to be heavy consumers of media about the election and had higher interest. They tended to influence opinion followers, or persons with lower media exposure, knowledge, and interest (Lowery & DeFluer, 1995).

The follow-up Decatur study looked specifically at the concept of the influence of opinion leaders within four decision-making areas of daily life: 1) Marketing, 2) fashion, 3) public affairs, and 4) movies. The study looked specifically at the buying habits of females. In short, the researchers uncovered that the following were three key factors in positioning someone as an opinion leader for those four decision-making areas: 1) Life cycle – is someone young and single, married with children, etc. – 2) position in the socioeconomic status of the community, and 3) social contacts. Said another way, opinion leaders tend to know a lot about a subject, have the financial and social resources to attain the subject, and are well-connected socially regarding that subject (Lowery & DeFluer, 1995).

In sum, the argument goes that while the media might be good at telling us about things, it is the people with whom we interact that influence our decision-making and opinions about those things.

Mind you, all of this was decades before the Internet and its offspring, social media. Social networking sites like Facebook (and Friendster before it) simply pioneered the mapping of interactions and influence[21]. No surprises then that companies soon began to hone in on who was influencing whom, realizing that when some people share something online, it has a greater effect on online action than when other people share something online.

Digital influence, then, is the online manifestation of the type of influence that was uncovered by scholars like Lazarsfeld, Katz, and colleagues in the 1940s. What's old is new again.

To learn more about digital influencers and influencer marketing, see Chapter 8 of Karen Freberg's *Social Media for Strategic Communication: Creative Strategies and Research-Based Applications.*

Why

Why are digital influencers so powerful in helping spread a message or drive sales? Your students can intuit this answer – most, if not all of them, follow influencers and a class discussion will illuminate the influencers that they like, why they look up to those influencers, and how those influencers have impacted their shopping decisions. So have that conversation.

After that, you may also want to point out the growing trends in influencer marketing to help illuminate the Why to your students. For example, a report by Socialbakers found that in just the first quarter of 2019, sponsored content has been published by 25,000 Instagram profiles, with the majority of those posts coming from influencers with less than 10,000 followers (Gesenhues, 2019b; "Must-Know Influencer Trends," 2019;).

The Talkwalker Global State of Influencer Marketing report released in March 2019 looked at over 800 PR and marketing professionals ("The global state of influencer marketing in 2019," 2019). It found that while 69% of respondents saw influencer marketing as a strategic priority and 61% intend to increase spending in influencer marketing, measuring return on investment (ROI), identifying impactful influencers, and coming up with creative ways to integrate influencers into campaigns were noted challenges.

Okay, so students have direct experience with influencers and they also are seeing influencer marketing as a rising trend. But how about some good old fashion communication theories and concepts? You may find it helpful to funnel the conversation into three concepts that will help illuminate why digital influencers tend to work more effectively than traditional top-down

---

[21] For a great listen at how Friendster pioneered online social network mapping, check out the episodes Friendster 1: The Rise, and Friendster 2: The Fall from the Startup Podcast here: https://gimletmedia.com/shows/startup/n8hogn
and here https://gimletmedia.com/shows/startup/8whow5.

promotion (and thus why digital influencers can be an effective part of a social media strategy). Those terms are: Change agent, heterophily, and homophily.

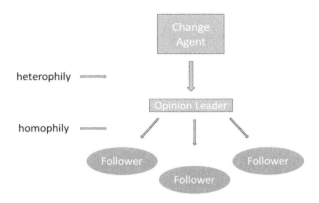

Image 5. The heterophily and homophily that tends to exist between change agents, opinion leaders, and opinion followers.

Digital influencers function as horizontal media in that the consumer and the media tend to be close in perceived social status, demographics, interests, and preferences. This is what makes digital influencers so valuable to brands. Public relations practitioners and marketers serve as change agents. They are not necessarily in the same social group of the people they wish to influence. The term change agents comes from the literature on diffusion of innovations theory (Rogers, 2003). This is an important theoretical framework for helping students think about how information spreads. Tell your students to think of a change agent as someone who seeks to influence whether an opinion leader does or does not adopt something new. A change agent tends to be quite different than the opinion leader and the opinion leader's followers. That is, change agents and opinion leaders and their followers tend to have a high degree of heterophily (see Image 5). On the other hand, opinion leaders and opinion followers tend to have high homophily; or simply put, they have a lot in common. At least, that's what the opinion follower thinks. And it is this perception that makes the opinion leader so relatable. But remember, as discovered in the research discussed above, opinion leaders are not exactly like the opinion followers: They have higher social status, greater knowledge and experience with the subject matter, and tend to be affable and gregarious. They have the 'cool kid at school' formula in their favor. Perhaps this is why digital influencers are so popularly used for aspirational promotions, such as lifestyle products, travel, and luxury goods.

No wonder so much money is being spent today on digital influencer marketing. They allow change agents to seamlessly insert their product or service into an existing community that the change agents would not otherwise have credibility in.

How

Once students understand why influencers are such a big trend, have explored how influencers impact their own decisions, and have learned about why influencers are effective at accelerating the adoptions change agents are advocating for, it is time to discuss how to identify influencers.

Of course, social media listening tools and other platforms can be used to identify influencers. But before your students hop on a computer, they need to first understand how to identify the right kind of influencer as well as how influencers can best be utilized. Further, they need to understand that the influencer space comes with many potential pitfalls.

Back in 2012, as digital influencers were getting noticed for their sales-generating and trend-setting abilities, Brian Solis (2012) wrote about three key pillars of digital influence which he defined as reach, relevance, and resonance. Reach is about relationships and how information can move across social groups. Relevance is about the affinity for the subject matter itself and the authority and trust the messenger brings to that subject matter. Resonance is the interaction occurring around the content, including the frequency, length of visibility and, engagement a network has with the content. While this report is over seven years old, the pillars remain an important consideration when thinking about how and why an idea spreads.

Below are some questions for students to think about when considering influencers. They are derived from the Solis report. But first, let's set up a brief activity.

Evaluating Influencers Activity

Have your students pick a few influencers. You can have them pick well-known influencers that they like and follow, have them do a quick Google search for top influencers, or you can find a list of influencers to share with them, such as:

- https://influencermarketinghub.com/top-25-instagram-influencers/.

Once picked, have your students work through the questions below. You will see a question followed by an activity to help students explore, think critically, and problem solve:

1. **Question:** Reach – Who is the influencer connected to and does the influencer have strong relationships with people in a given social group?
    a. **Activity:** Tell your students they need to beware of influencer

fraud as it is a growing concern. Some would-be-influencers are buying fake followers and likes. Other would-be-influencers will use the follow-unfollow technique, where they will follow a lot of people in the hope that these people will follow them back. The person will then unfollow these individuals, giving a false impression that they have a high follower count compared to the total number of people that they follow. This is a technique to game the follow/follower ratio, or the number of followers one has in comparison to the total number of people one follows. When one has a high ratio of followers to the number of accounts followed, it is sometimes seen as a sign that one is influential – although this is not necessarily the case. Captiv8 and Horizon Media have partnered to help verify talent (Raji, 2019) and Likewise is an AI-powered tool launched in 2019 which aims to help marketers identify fake influencers (Field, 2019). Have your students dig through and examine an influencer's followers to see how they interact with others. Have your students look at the followers of those followers. Do their interactions seem human and genuine, or is there not much below the surface? Are any interactions happening between your influencer's followers or are the posts primarily generic comments? These are not fool-proof ways to identify potential influencer fraud, but they will get your students looking under the hood and thinking about these concerns.

2. **Questions:** Relevance - Is there evidence that the influencer's opinions are trusted by the influencer's followers? Is there evidence that the influencer is seen as an authority on the topic?

   a. **Activity:** Again, have your students dig through the interactions that followers have with an influencer. The students should be looking for signals that the influencer is actually influencing the opinions or decisions of their followers. Now, your students don't have access to any tools that would show a sales funnel, such as a follower clicking a link and going to buy a pair of sneakers. But, there may be evidence in the comments that the influencer is affecting the awareness, interest, or opinions of followers. For example, a quick scroll through posts on account of Instagram influencer @chiaraferragni shows numerous comments and questions from her followers inquiring about a dress she is wearing in a particular post, indicating that the followers are interested in the product itself (see: https://www.instagram.com/p/BwZSiQLhJTo/).

3. **Questions:** Resonance – How often is this influencer being talked about online? For how long does the conversation around their posted content appear to last? How much engagement does the influencer get on their posts?

a. **Activity:** Have your students search the influencer's name or handle on Google and on appropriate social media to see if others are talking about the influencer. Have your students look over the influencer's engagement for the last 10 posts. Is engagement consistent? Have your students dig into a few posts. If there are timestamps available, have them see if the audience engagement is spread out across time or bundled together. These small actions will get your students thinking about the influencer's resonance.

The influencer landscape faces many challenges relating to ethics, credibility, and legal issues. The landscape around working with influencers is somewhat murky as it is an emergent field. This is why ethical behavior is so very important. Documentaries such as *Fyre: The Greatest Party that Never Happened* and *Fyre Fraud,* discussed above, have exposed a slew of concerns regarding deception and to what extent influencers are responsible for the products they endorse. But there are many other cases and considerations. Influencers who are seen as inauthentic or deceptive may quickly find that their followers have turned on them. For example, a vegan influencer was ousted for reportedly deceiving her audience when it was revealed that she ate fish and eggs for health reasons (Rosenberg, 2019). Alternatively, there are those who question whether influencers are actually influential. Because just about anyone can say they are an influencer, there are plenty of so-called influencers who do not deliver much in the way of value for a brand. Gianluca Casaccia, who co-owns a beach club in the Philippines, went viral when he called out travelers on his Facebook page for trying to claim influencer status in an attempt to get free food and lodging (Murphy, 2019). Further, there are legal considerations around working with influencers. For example, an influencer needs to provide transparency to their followers when they are being compensated to post about a product or service. A failure to tag a post as promoted is seen as a violation of advertising disclosure rules as it may mislead the public ("The FTC's endorsement guidelines," 2017).

Philip Trippenbach, head of influencer at Edelman UK, believes that influencers are best used when there is a strong overlap between the influencer and the brand (Hickman, 2018). According to an article in PRWeek, Trippenbach does not believe that using influencers to push products is an effective tactic, although it is a highly popular tactic. Brand-level marketing trumps product-level promotion, in his view, because it showcases how brands can empower influencers in their areas of specialty. He cites a PayPal campaign, #PoletoPole, where travel vloggers used PayPal during their travels to showcase how the service can be used to go cashless while traveling. This, Trippenbach argues, is more effective than a disruptive ad post where an influencer pushes a product, such as a soda, that is not in line with that influencer's specialty.

Influencer/Brand Fit Activity

You may want to share some of the above examples or other relevant examples with your students and discuss them. Then, with the above in mind, brainstorm some other questions with your students that they need to consider when looking for influencer/brand fit. Some might include:

1. What makes this influencer a good fit for us?
2. Does this influencer's behavior align with our brand image?
3. What are the influencer's values and do they align with our brand's values?
4. How could we integrate our brand naturally into this influencer's specialty – that is, what this influencer does and is known for?
5. What is our ask – that is, what exactly do we want this influencer to do and are they capable of delivering?
6. What will it cost to work with this influencer, can we afford it, and is it worth it to us given our ask?
7. Can the influencer share with us any case studies of how they have worked with brands like ours to drive the actions we are looking for?

Of course, the most important conversation is about why the client wishes to work with influencers to begin with. Questions may include: What are our goals for working with influencers? Are we trying to 1) drive brand or product awareness, 2) establish reputation, authority, and credibility, 3) rebuild trust, 4) sell products or services, or 5) something else? This is the conversation that a brand should start with. Working with an influencer because it is a hot trend is not a strategy.

Tools for Finding Digital Influencers

With the above in mind, take a few minutes to explain to your students what kind of influencers they are looking for. Recall, the purpose of the class-wide project is to run the social media for a client, such as your academic department. Ergo, the influencers you are going to have your students look for are likely those that can help share your client's social media content and thus spread awareness of your client. You may also be trying to use those influencers to establish your client as an authority.

Once you have had a conversation with your students about the types of influencers they should be looking for, it is time to teach them to find influencers. There are many tools that you can use, both paid and free. Some popular paid tools include:

Name	Link
Talkwalker's Influencer One	https://www.talkwalker.com/influencer-one
Buzzsumo	https://buzzsumo.com/
Followerwonk	https://followerwonk.com/
Captiv8	https://captiv8.io/product-platform/
GroupHigh	https://www.grouphigh.com/
Meltwater's Influencer Product	https://www.meltwater.com/find-influencers/

Additionally, Meltwater and other social listening software programs (such as those discussed in Chapter 4) have features that you can use to look for influencers.

Both Buzzsumo and Followerwonk offer free versions of their software, which come with limited searches and features. These tools may be less precise, but they are good for teaching your students to find influencers.

Name	Link
Followerwonk's free tool	https://followerwonk.com/bio
Buzzsumo's free tool	http://app.buzzsumo.com/influencers

Each free tool offers different affordances and thus the means of finding influencers may vary. For example, the free version of Followerwonk enables you to search Twitter by name, location, URL, or keywords. A search for the keyword 'lacrosse' for example will produce a list of accounts with the word lacrosse in the bio. You can sort results by Followerwonk's social authority score (Followerwonk's proprietary influence scoring system[22]), follower account, number of accounts followed, total tweets, and account age. Meltwater's social listening software enables you to sort your social media searches by a post's reach, engagement and prominence.

More advanced paid tools offer more precise and granular data about potential influencers and their relevance to your market. For example, the free Followerwonk tool does not allow you to dig into the account and look more deeply at engagement with that account's posts. But the paid version does. Because of the limitations of free tools, it may be helpful to triangulate influencer research by using several tools.

Inform your students of these limitations. When they do influencer research, then, they will not be looking at proof of influence. Rather, they will be looking for potential indicators of influence – such as reach, social authority score, follower count, etc. Critical thinking and analytic skills will be important to interpreting what these indicators mean. Just because

---

[22] Read more about the Followerwonk social authority score and how it is calculated here: https://moz.com/blog/social-authority

someone has a high follower count does not mean that the person is influential on a given topic. The questions and activities in the Evaluating Influencers Activity on the previous pages will be useful in helping students evaluate the potential influencers that they find through the tools we have discussed.

Do and Reflect

The Content Period 1 assignment (see the full assignment in the chapter appendix) asks students to identify a list of influencers that they can work with and incorporate into their content strategy. Students are asked to provide evidence and reasoning to support their list of proposed influencers. You may want your students to work with these influencers just during the Content Period 1, or throughout all of the content periods. It's up to you. But, be sure that students understand that they are expected to reach out to these influencers and attempt to incorporate them into their content. Before you set your students off to begin working on identifying influencers, here are a few things to keep in mind that may help you provide guidance to your students.

When brands work with influencers, there is often an expectation of compensation. Depending on the nature of your class client, this may not be a viable option. For example, in my social media class, the students are promoting our academic department. The context is a much smaller scale. We do not offer influencers any tangible incentives, financial or otherwise, for their participation. We have never had an issue with that as we are an educational program and our influencers are very understanding of that. According to Karen Freberg (2018), not all influencers expect financial compensation or free access to products or services. Experience, goodwill, opportunities to share, growth of one's influence, and association with well-recognized brands or entities can all serve as compensation to an influencer (Freberg, 2018).

While many of us have come to think of influencers as synonymous with the promotion of products and services, recall that there are other ways in which one can act as an influencer. If your client is an academic department or other entity within your university, then your class is likely seeking influencers who are brand fans that can lend their reputation and enthusiasm to increase awareness and/or further the credibility and reputation of the program.

Here are just a few ways that your students may creatively incorporate influencers into their content plans:

1. Social media takeovers and vlogs.
2. Re-sharing your client's content with or without comments.
3. Testimonials.
4. Mentions and shout outs.

5.   Interviews.
6.   Collaborations between your client and other organizations.
7.   Spotlights.

Encourage your students to consider how they can work with influencers. It may help them brainstorm possible influencers. For example, in fall 2018, the Twitter group in my class worked with a senior in our department who had over 160,000 followers on his YouTube channel. They wanted to work with him because he is well known not only on our campus but also among many teens and college-aged people. The student is known for his video game videos and commentary and has a lot of experience in the video space. The student agreed to make a brief video testimonial discussing why he chose to major in communication, what he has gained from his experience, and how that has helped him succeed. This student tweeted out the video and our department retweeted it. It became the Twitter group's most engaged post of the semester.

Next, help your students think about ways to approach the target influencers. Working with influencers should be mutually beneficial. The first step should be to engage with and share the influencer's content. All communication should be professional, kind, courteous and authentic. Influencers are more likely to work with students if they have an emotional connection with your class client and if they believe their followers will also love it. The YouTube case above is a great example of that. Influencers are also often looking to expand their own reach and grow their audience. Based on your class client, there may be an opportunity to help the influencer in this regard. There also may be a way to help add to the influencer's credibility and reputation. One way to do this is to feature the influencer's expertise in a piece of content. If your client works in an area that is near and dear to the influencer's heart, say pets or education, then offering the influencer an opportunity to give back to that cause could be another recruiting incentive.

Let your students know that not all influencers are going to contact them back, and that's okay. Not all influencers are going to be a good fit. I do not penalize my students for failing to succeed in their attempts to work with influencers. But I expect them to reach out to the influencers and make the attempt. There is a lot to be learned in that effort.

Lastly, here are a few common pitfalls that I have run into with this assignment that you should be aware of:

1.   Students may think too big for the client – Because many students are very familiar with famous influencers, they may hope to work with influences that are off-brand or realistically out of reach for the client you are working with. If your class client is your academic department's social media or is a client in a small market or is a small business, it is unlikely that a celebrity influencer will work with them. This is particularly true because your students may not have much to offer that

influencer in terms of payment or other incentives. Set realistic expectations for your students.

2. Students may just rely on their friends – If your class client is your academic department, then your students likely know people at the university or within your department who are influential among their peers on or offline. Such students may actually be a great fit – after all, college students are often influenced by their peers. Encourage your students when they think of such influencers. They aren't being lazy. They are using their analytical abilities to determine who would be a good fit for their audience and their client. But here are a few suggestions. First, I suggest that you do not let any student in your class serve as an influencer. Require your students to find influencers outside of the class. Second, always require students to show evidence and reasoning to support their case for why someone is an appropriate influencer. Third, require your students to have more than just other students serve as influencers – who else around campus and/or the community influences the students? Perhaps campus clubs, sports, the student affairs office, SGA, or other entities are influential. Fourth, even though your students may be able to brainstorm appropriate influencers without the use of software tools to help them, require the students to do these searches regardless so they can get practice.

With the above in mind, set your students to work on building their influencer list and go around the room to help them. This is the perfect time to chat with student groups to help them reflect upon the influencers they are considering and to guide them towards appropriate influencers. Bring up issues of influencer/client fit. Ask students what public disclosure they have in mind when dealing with influencers and how they can ensure their dealings are ethical, transparent, and within FTC guidelines.

Drilldown: Best Practices for Creating Social Media Content

You've got your students working on creating content. But how do they create great content? How do you teach the techniques of social media content creation?

In addition to the list of resources I provided in Chapter 5 that your students can use in creating content, I want to talk about a few best practices that you may want to create brief lessons about or that you can assign as homework. It is beyond the scope of this book to cover all of the digital and multimedia techniques that students can learn.

Further, there simply isn't enough time in a social media class to teach all of the skills of content production.

Ideally, the social media class is a place to take the multimedia creation skills honed in other classes and organize and focus them into strategic planning and execution. If your department, or another department on campus, offers courses on writing, audio, videography, photography, graphic design, special effects, and other multimedia skills, I suggest that you strongly encourage your students to take those. You may even want to require some such courses as prerequisites. Fortunately, in my department we have very talented faculty who teach these skills and students come into my social media class with a diverse array of strengths in multimedia that I can leverage. As I have discussed earlier in this book, you do not need every student to be an expert at every applicable skillset. If you have a mixture of skills in each group, then this is sufficient. You just need to be able to leverage the skillsets students do have and encourage them to learn new skills or develop existing ones along the way.

I know that not all of you who are reading this are fortunate to have an array of multimedia-focused classes offered at your university. In such cases, it is a worthy long-term goal to work towards building these into your curriculum. A very strong case can be made to your department chair or dean for this need. But alas, this is easier said than done.

While I said above that I view this class as a way to add a strategic mindset to multimedia skills honed in other classes, I am very aware that you may be in a position where you have to manage both teaching strategic skills and multimedia skills. I hope the below resources will help you work towards these goals by providing best practices for content creation.

Social Media Copy

There are lots of great resources for helping your students write better social media copy. Social Media Today provides a great list (Goldschein, 2019):

1. Write the way you talk.
2. Write consistently.
3. Write first, then edit heavily.
4. Read your competitors' feeds.
5. Provide value with every post.
6. Conduct hashtag and keyword research (but don't let terms drive all your content).
7. Write to your target demographic.
8. Write short for engagement and long for traffic.
9. Add visual elements to your post.

Because article headlines, Facebook posts, LinkedIn updates, and tweets have a lot in common, I am going to discuss them as a group. They all seek to quickly grab the reader's attention and drive a behavior. Often, a tweet or Facebook post is designed to elicit a link click, a share or retweet, or a like. An article headline aims to entice the reader to start reading the article.

While Twitter doubled the Tweet length in 2017 from 140 to 280 characters, brevity remains central to Twitter posts. According to Tech Crunch, only 12% of tweets are more than 140 characters, and only 5% are more than 190 characters (Perez, 2018). Similarly, shorter posts perform better on Facebook. With 50 characters or less the recommended length according to BuzzSumo (Moeller, 2019). LinkedIn status updates should be in this same range (Jackson, n.d.).

Teaching students to write succinct headlines or social posts that drive action is key. The 4U rule from the American Writers & Artist Association is a good one to teach:

1. Unique – What is different about your message?
2. Urgent – Why does your message matter to the audience right now?
3. Useful – How will it help your audience?
4. Unambiguous – What is ultra-specific and clear about this message?

Having your students evaluate headlines, tweets or Facebook posts for the 4Us is a great exercise. Having your students evaluate one another's writing is also a great exercise.

There are many headline formulas that content marketers have used over the years, which can serve as tweets as well. These formulas may seem, well formulaic, but they can help your students develop an eye for what grabs attention. Here are two that I like:

1. SUMO - https://sumo.com/stories/headline-formulas
2. Buffer - https://buffer.com/library/headline-formulas

In addition to the above, a Tweet should often have a call to action (CTA) or leave the reader wanting more. A CTA tells the reader what you want them to do, such as click a link, sign up for a newsletter, etc. A CTA is only effective to the extent that the offer it follows is compelling. The offer, in this case, is the text that comes before it in the tweet. Another technique is to use mystery to create an information gap. An information gap occurs when people identify an uncomfortable gap in knowledge and are motivated to reduce this discomfort by taking an action (e.g., clicking an article link) (Heath & Heath, 2007). A tweet that gives just enough but withholds something the reader will want to know can be effective for getting users to click. You have seen this technique used in clickbait, a la the listicle that uses the "you won't believe what number five is" approach. A less spammy post might read: "14 reasons to stop shoveling your driveway when it snows" (Jeez, I hate shoveling. If I had an army of evidence for why I shouldn't shovel, perhaps I could win my partner over to my way of thinking). Or, try: "The Smiths thought it was a good idea to shovel their driveway. Then they learned about shovel-free living" (Shovel-free living, that sounds like a lifestyle I can embrace). You get the idea. Just leave a gap that you fulfill when the user takes the desired action. Remember, clickbait does not deliver on its promises.

Make sure the content your students create does deliver.

Lastly, hashtags are a critical tool for any social media platform. Using relevant hashtags can help others find your content. For example, LinkedIn users can subscribe to hashtags of interest. Hashtag research was touched on in Chapter 4 when we covered social media listening. Hashtag research can be done via the search tools on native platforms as well as through tools like Meltwater. Other tools such as Hashtagify (https://hashtagify.me) and Keyhole (https://keyhole.co) and RiteTag (https://ritetag.com) can also be useful. By monitoring relevant online conversations, one can find commonly used hashtags to employ.

Facebook

According to data analyzed by BuzzSumo, video receives the most engagement on Facebook, followed by photos (Moeller, 2019). Shorter video – between three and five minutes - is recommended. You can read the full report on best practices here:

- https://buzzsumo.com/blog/facebook-engagement-guide/

Twitter

Tweets with photos or videos perform better and when discussing best practices for creating Twitter content, it is important to emphasize this. Twitter Business has developed a list of best practices to check out:

- https://business.twitter.com/en/basics/what-to-tweet.html.

Instagram Posts

Instagram is widely loved for the beautiful artwork and photography its members share. The community expects posts to be high-quality and well-edited. While professional photography equipment such as a DSLR or mirrorless camera is preferred, today's smartphone cameras are more than sufficient to produce great Instagram-ready content. Composition, lighting, content, and focus are all important factors for producing excellent Instagram photography, according to Bruna Camargo (Camargo, n.d.). In this great tutorial, Camargo provides simple tips for improving one's photography:

- https://www.ignitesocialmedia.com/instagram-marketing-2/photography-community-managers-get-fans-double-tap/.

Hootsuite also has a great guide for taking better photos:

- https://blog.hootsuite.com/how-to-take-good-instagram-photos/.

Don't forget the editing. Paid software editing tools, such as the Adobe Creative Cloud, are highly useful. Additionally, see the list of free editing tools listed on page 87 of the print edition of this book.

Story Posts: Facebook, Instagram and Snapchat

Story posts on Facebook, Instagram and Snapchat are generally informal and often playful, frequently accompanied by stickers, text, or doodles. I like to think of story posts as a behind-the-scenes vantage – they are more intimate and in a sense less guarded.

If a team in your class is planning to put together a series of stories, the team should storyboard them out. Storyboarding, a technique often used in mapping out visual productions such as movies, is simply a sketched out plan for a succession of frames - visual scenes or images. Hootsuite provides a step-by-step guide for storyboarding social media stories as well as templates for doing so:

- https://blog.hootsuite.com/storyboard-instagram-stories/.

Facebook published an update to its Instagram Creators Guide in April, 2019. It contains a series of tips for engaging one's audience on Instagram through the feed, stories and live features, as well as through IGTV, Instagram's section for long-form video:

- https://www.facebook.com/creators/discover/instagram-creator-guide.

Video and Livestreaming

Livestreaming is very popular on many social platforms including Facebook, YouTube and Instagram. LinkedIn announced a livestreaming feature in early 2019 (Lunden, 2019).

When it comes to strategy, check out Facebook's 2018 guide to video strategy:

- https://www.facebook.com/creators/discover/upgrade-your-video-strategy.

Proper lighting, microphone quality, and Internet speed are all important factors for a successful livestream. Have your students set up the camera ahead of time and practice framing the camera so that the viewer sees the people and things that you want in the frame. Do a practice recording to ensure lighting and sound are working properly.

For mobile streaming, tools like tripods and gimbals are best for avoiding a shaky camera. Selfie sticks are inexpensive and a good alternative. While people will often forgive poor video quality, they will not be so forgiving of bad sound. Computer and phone microphones are often sufficient. If possible, opt for higher quality microphones. Inexpensive, quality USB microphones can be purchased through sites like Amazon. For lighting of one's face on a livestream, ring lights are recommended, though a professor's desk lamp can be a free alternative.

While livestreaming can be done with great success directly through social media platforms, third-party tools can be used to increase production value. Such tools can allow users to place text overlay on the video stream, switch between multiple camera angles, and more. Open Broadcaster Software (https://obsproject.com/) is a free tool that can be used to achieve many of these effects. However, you may find that it is more challenging to learn to use than streamlined paid alternatives.

As public relations professor and founder and host of the Facebook live show Classrooms Without Walls, Ai Addyson-Zhang notes, technology is the least important aspect of your show. Addyson-Zhang writes that when asked what kit to use to start a livestreaming show, her answer is "whatever you have right now!" (Addyson-Zhang, 2019, ¶ 15).

Addyson-Zhang provides the following tips for success hosting a livestreamed show (Addyson-Zhang, 2019):

1. Message – Content quality is key and its relevance for the target audience.
2. Consistency – Content needs to be produced on a regular, pre-determined schedule because it takes time to build an audience.
3. Development – Respond to your audience and grow where opportunity presents itself.
4. Technology – Successful livestreaming can be done with an Internet connection and a smartphone. Technology can be upgraded over time. That's why technology takes a backseat to quality content. Start with what you have and upgrade as the circumstances allow.

If you are not livestreaming but instead shooting video to be published later, increase its production value by editing it. While paid editing tools may be preferred, there are free options. YouTube provides a free online editing suite in its YouTube Studio. Both Mac and Windows come with basic editing software. See the list of free video editing software on page 87 of the print edition of this book. Open Broadcaster Software can also be used for enhancing video recording.

Drilldown: Contests and Giveaways

One way that companies try to spread awareness or increase engagement is through contests or giveaways on social media. Many small businesses do this in an attempt to create a network effect in which fans post content, such as photos with a product, to help spread awareness of the product through the fans' networks. Many large businesses do this as a way to engage their fans or promote new products. Brands from Kettle Brand, to Ruffwear, to Absolut have used some form of giveaway to engage their audience.

While social media contests and giveaways may not be as effective as they once were (Carter, 2017) and limited research suggests that contests are not associated with increased shares, likes, and comments (Quesenberry & Coolsen, 2018), they remain a draw due to their relative ease and low cost. With organic engagement falling on many social platforms, contests and giveaways can be a fun way to boost engagement.

That's why, for the last few years, I have incorporated a contest into the Content Period 1 assignment in my classes. It's also a very fun way to jump start the content creation process and get students engaged in the class. Further, student groups sometimes struggle to come up with content ideas for Content Period 1. This assignment provides a nice jump start because it gives the students a subject to focus on since, as I will explain below, I allow the content they create for the contest to count towards their required content totals for Content Period 1.

Below, I will provide a brief overview of how I incorporate this contest and why (find the optional contest assignment in the chapter appendix).

Because I teach the social media assignment in the fall, the contest has always been about Halloween. For my class, the syllabus aligns in such a way that Halloween tends to fall the week after Content Period 1 is due. Thus, Content Period 1 is a great time period for students to create promotional content for the contest. However, you could make the contest about any trend – think of an upcoming movie release like *Avengers: Endgame* – or special date – think Valentine's Day, Thanksgiving, midterms, #teacherappreciationday, etc.

We have done costume contests, pumpkin carving contests, and a candy decorating contest. Students have come up with a host of other fun ideas as well. I have found, however, that the costume contest gets the most engagement, probably because the students are already dressing up for Halloween and thus the threshold for participation is lowered. This brings forth an important point. Participation in contests is a high-threshold engagement, meaning it requires a high level of engagement from users – content creation. Contrast that with applause (e.g., likes), which is a very-low-threshold engagement and amplification (e.g., retweeting), which is a low-threshold engagement. The higher the threshold, the more resources, such as time, energy, and skills, it takes to participate. Like a pyramid, many people will engage in very-low-threshold and low-threshold engagement, fewer people will engage in mid-threshold engagement – such as comments – and even fewer people will engage in high-threshold engagement. Thus, expect relatively lower levels of engagement with your contest.

As a class, we discuss the days we want the contest to run and when we will announce the winner. Using those dates, I provide students with the rules for the contest which they can use in creating promotional content. The rules can be found on the contest assignment in the chapter appendix.

As explained in the assignment instructions, each group is required to make at least one post promoting the class contest. Students are strongly encouraged to create more content and I will count up to three posts (except for the blog, which I will only count up to one post) about the contest towards their required Content Period 1 content total.

I have always held the contest exclusively on Instagram given its focus on photos, but this may limit participation. We have used all of our other platforms to promote the contest. We have used a Twitter poll to decide the winner. We have tried both hashtags and account tagging as the means for participants to submit their entry. Both have their limitations, but I always require that entries use a hashtag with the word contest in it to conform with disclosure requirements about giveaways. For example, we have used #shepcommcontest in the past.

To incentivize participation, I always buy a fun custom coffee mug designed for our department that I fill with Halloween candy. It costs me about $12. I let the students take a photo of the prize to use in promotion. You could even team up with other departments or organizations on campus or in your local community to cross-promote the contest or even turn it into a fundraiser.

While it is the responsibility of the students to come up with ways to promote the contest, here are some potential ideas to have in your back pocket which you can use to help inspire students if they are having a hard time understanding what you are looking for:

1. Have students create their own entries and submit them as examples to create a bandwagon effect (don't let them win though and be sure to have students be transparent that their entries are just for fun).
2. Show the prize participants can win.
3. Countdowns.
4. Find ways to get different groups (e.g., clubs, Greek life) on campus to participate as a way to 'win for the team.'
5. Reminders and nudges throughout the contest.
6. Showcase winners from a prior year.

As a class, my students and I pick out our favorite four submissions during the class period after Halloween. Someone in the Twitter group creates a poll with the four entries and the winner is decided via the public poll (note that I do not count this as part of their Content Period 1 content. It is simply a quick in-class ask). The trick to running a Twitter poll with a photo is to tweet the photo and then retweet it as a poll.

Image 6. The 2018 #ShepCommContest Twitter poll to decide the Halloween costume contest winner. Note that the poll is a retweet of the original tweet containing the image.

Recommended Readings and More

Documentaries

Note: The below documentaries contain content that is not suitable for all audiences. Viewers may find the content offensive.

Furst, J. (Director), Nason, J.W. (Director). (2019). *Fyre Fraud* [Motion Picture]. United States of America: Hulu.

Marcus, B. (Director). (2018). *The American Meme* [Motion Picture]. France: Bert Marcus Productions.

Smith, C. (Director). (2019). Fyre: The Greatest Party that Never Happened [Motion Picture]. United States of America: Library Films.

Podcasts

Friendster 1: The Rise. (2017, April 21). *Startup*. Retrieved from https://gimletmedia.com/shows/startup/n8hogn.

Friendster 2: The Fall (2017, April 28). *Startup*. Retrieved from https://gimletmedia.com/shows/startup/8whow5.

Readings

Addyson-Zhang, A. (2019, April 18). Using livestreaming to grow your brand, community, & influence. *Shonali Burke*. Retrieved from https://shonaliburke.com/using-livestreaming-to-grow-your-brand-community-influence/.

Camargo, B. (n.d.). Instagram photography for community managers: How to get fans to double-tap that. *Ignite social media*. Retrieved from https://www.ignitesocialmedia.com/instagram-marketing-2/photography-community-managers-get-fans-double-tap/.

Cyca, M. (2018, September 12). How to take good Instagram photos on your phone: A step-by-step guide. *Hootsuite*. Retrieved from https://blog.hootsuite.com/how-to-take-good-instagram-photos/.

Freberg, K. (2018). *Social Media for Strategic Communication*. Thousand Oaks, CA: Sage Publications, Inc.

Goldschein, E. (2019, March 24). The non-writers' guide to writing better social media copy. *Social Media Today*. Retrieved from https://www.socialmediatoday.com/news/the-non-writers-guide-to-writing-better-social-media-copy/551143/.

Instagram creator guide. (2019, April 25). *Facebook*. Retrieved from https://www.facebook.com/creators/discover/instagram-creator-guide.

Moeller, S. (2019, January 3). The 2019 ultimate guide to Facebook engagement. *Buzzsumo*. Retrieved from https://buzzsumo.com/blog/facebook-engagement-guide/.

Solis, B. (2012). *The rise of digital influence*. San Mateo, C.A.: Altimer Group.

The FTC's endorsement guides: What people are asking. (2017). *Federal Trade Commission*. Retrieved from https://www.ftc.gov/tips-advice/business-center/guidance/ftcs-endorsement-guides-what-people-are-asking.

Upgrade your video strategy. (2018, October 15). *Facebook*. Retrieved from https://www.facebook.com/creators/discover/upgrade-your-video-strategy.

What to tweet. (n.d.). *Twitter Business*. Retrieved from https://business.twitter.com/en/basics/what-to-tweet.html.

Chapter 6 Appendix

Content Period 1 Assignment

Note to the reader: Provide the Social Media Brand Guidelines to your students (see the Chapter 5 Appendix). These are the same guidelines they should have used in creating their strategic briefs. Recall that the Social Media Grading Rubric can be distributed to students to guide them in creating their content. In fact, I attach it to the bottom of the assignment when I distribute the assignment to my students. You can use it to assist in grading (see the Chapter 5 Appendix).

In the below assignment, modify the time period for which you want the students creating proposed content based on your needs.

The instructions tell the students to organize their content using the content calendar the professor will provide. This is a reference to the Social Media Content Calendar Template referenced in the Chapter 5 Appendix. Make a shareable copy with your students with updated dates to reflect the weeks for which your students will be creating content.

Lastly, recall the list of resources provided in Chapter 5 which may help students in designing their social media content (see p. 87).

Overview

Purpose
For Content Period 1, your team will create 1 **batch** (see definition below) of content which can be spread out <u>over a 3-week period during the 9th, 10th, and 11th week of the semester.</u>

To Do
1. Relying on your Strategic Brief, and any feedback you received, create content for your social channel for the above-listed time period. Consider any dates, events, or other tie ins on the calendar for that time frame (e.g., Thanksgiving, Fall break, etc.).
2. Create a list of 3-4 proposed key digital influencers – and evidence (e.g., screen shots) with a sentence or two for why you chose them.

Content Tasks
You have two tasks:
1. **Content Requirements (Quality > quantity)**
Organized for the time period assigned on the social media content calendar.

My primary concerns are:
- Each piece of content ties together – it is purposive and fits with the plan you created in your strategic brief assignment.
- You've created audience centric, original content that will stand out.
- It's of a high professional quality (writing, editing, visuals, etc.).

Content Period 1 Batch =
- Blogs: 3 posts – About 1/2 page to 3/4 page double spaced text. Minimum of 2 visuals per post needed.
  - For each post you need to provide 2 different promotional tweets. Write these in the content calendar on the day that you want your blog to be published and the day after.
- Instagram, Twitter, Snapchat: 7 posts of ORIGINAL visuals and text.

2. Proposed Influencers
Produce a list of 3-4 digital influencers that you would like to work with on your social media platform (Note: The blog team may use influencers from other social platforms).

- Provide image evidence of each influencer's status (e.g., screen grab of their audience size, reach, authority score on Followerwonk, etc.)
- 1-2 sentence rationale for why each is an appropriate digital influencer.

Considerations:
- Just because potential influencers have a high "authority score" or showed up on a search doesn't mean they are right for our client.
- Check out the profile, retweets, who they are interacting with, etc.
  - What are they posting about?
  - Who are they influencing, and is that our target public?
    - See their followers and importantly who they are interacting with (check those people's profiles)
- What are their interests?
  - Are they interested in / invested in our subject?
  - Are they already talking about it? What's their attitude towards it?
- Are they an attainable influencer, given our client?

Grading Criteria
- Appropriateness of work to the situation, audience, and client.
- Professional quality of content.
- Extent to which content is consistent with project goals.
- Extent to which content is consistent with team's strategy as put forth in their strategic brief.
- Considers/adapts to feedback given by professor.

Presentation Tasks

Your group will present your content to the class.
Time: About 6 minutes of presentation time.

Be sure to address:
1. Content
   a. How your content fits with your content categories (i.e., your 'content buckets').
   b. How your content takes into consideration any feedback you received from your strategic brief (from the professor's grading and class feedback).
2. Influencers
   a. Who they are, what your evidence and reasoning is for choosing them.
   b. How you plan to incorporate them into your content and why you think this will work as it relates to the goals and objectives put forward in your strategic brief and/or your content categories.

Q&A / Evaluation
Afterwards, your classmates (who are roleplaying as the client) will evaluate your presentation and will be encouraged to ask you questions.

Expectations
This is a casual presentation. Not all members have to speak, but they must be present in class on that day and join the team at the podium or they will receive -10% of the group's grade.

Social Media Contest Assignment

Overview

Required Content: The content you create for the social media contest will count towards the total pieces of content that your team is required to create for Content Period 1. Up to 3 of the posts you make (or 1 blog post for the blog team) will count towards the batch requirements listed in the Content Period 1 assignment.

Organize the content into your content calendar.

Contest Instructions
Use the below instructions when creating any promotional content:

Dates: Oct 24 through noon Nov. 1.
The winner will be announced Tuesday, Nov. 6.
Contest Hashtag: #shepcommcontest

Contest Name: ShepComm Halloween Costume Contest
Instructions:
- Post a photo of your Halloween costume on Instagram using #shepcommcontest. Submission deadline is noon, Nov. 1.
- Vote for your favorite submission via our Twitter poll at @ShepComm on Nov 1st.
- The winner will be announced on social media on Nov. 6.
- The contest is open to all students, faculty and staff at #ShepherdU

Content Period Presentation Assignment Feedback Form

Instructions:
Rank each on a scale of 1-7, where 1 means "strongly disagree" and 7 means "strongly agree." Look at the overall presentation as a whole, as opposed to individual students.

Question	Score:
Content	
If I saw this content being published by our client, I'd be proud to say I helped create it.	_____
The content is consistent with what they proposed in the past.	_____
This is professional work on par with work I'd expect from a professional and admired organization.	_____
Goals and Objectives	
Their content fits within the goals and objectives for the class project.	_____
Audience	
Excellent job considering audience needs, wants and desires.	_____
Excellent job creating content that audience would find compelling.	_____
Themes	_____
Content fit very well into our campaign's theme.	
Content fit very well into the class content themes (the calendar of themes).	_____
Improvement:	
Their content is (7) Better, (1) Worse, (3-4) About the same as what I saw at their last presentation.	_____

Written Comments: Considering the criteria above and other considerations you find important, please provide written feedback:

Which of their examples (if any) do you:

Suggest we publish: _____   Suggest we don't publish

Matthew J. Kushin, Ph.D.

CHAPTER 7: UNIT 5. CONTENT PERIOD 2, SOCIAL MEDIA METRICS, AND ONGOING SOCIAL LISTENING

The fifth unit of the semester focuses on social media metrics and ongoing social listening. Students begin monitoring metrics for the class client as part of the Content Period 2 assignment.

By this point in the semester, students have completed Content Period 1, presented it to the class, and submitted it to you for grading and possible publication on social media. As a reminder, you will be publishing the content from Unit 4 (Content Period 1) during the time period that you are teaching Unit 5 (Content Period 2). It is now time to have students work on Content Period 2, which will follow the same format as Content Period 1. However, students will be learning new skills and abilities during Content Period 2. Namely, students will learn about social media metrics. They will also build upon the social media listening skills that were introduced in Unit 2 (see Chapter 4).

Suggested Schedule: Weeks 8, 9 and 10

1. Day 15: Assignment Overview and Introducing Social Media Metrics
2. Day 16: Social Media Metrics: Planning and Metrics Goals Lecture and Metrics Lab Time
3. Day 17: Content Optimization Lecture and Optimization Lab Time
4. Day 18: Social Media Listening and Listening Lab Time
5. Day 19: Content Period 2 Lab Day
6. Day 20: Student Presentations

Unit Learning Objectives

1. Teach students the skills and abilities to gather and analyze social media metrics.
2. Introduce students to content optimization.
3. Enable students to build on the social media listening skills they developed in Unit 2 through ongoing social media listening.

Content Period 2 Assignment

The Content Period 2 Assignment is available in the chapter appendix below. Go over the assignment with your students. Recall that the teams will be required to present their content to the class. There is a presentation evaluation sheet in the Chapter 6 appendix, which you can have your students complete for the purpose of facilitating feedback.

The What, Why, How, Do, Reflect

Learning Objective 1: Social Media Metrics

What and Why

Numbers matter. Consider it a sign of the times. Whether motivated by pressure from upper management or a desire to understand one's performance and improve, students need to learn how to track, interpret, and analyze social media data. Social media metrics is a broad term to define the process of evaluating an array of measurable activities (i.e., data) on social media that impact a company's revenue[23].

In short, social media metrics are key to tracking the outcomes and successes of a campaign.

Each social media platform provides (or fails to provide) its own metrics to users. In some cases, a business profile is needed to get metrics. For example, a free Instagram Business account (https://www.facebook.com/business/profiles) or a free Facebook Creator Studio account (http://facebook.com/creatorstudio) is needed to access Instagram Insight metrics.

This blog post by Sprout Social provides a thorough look at the metrics available across many popular social media platforms. I encourage you to assign it as reading to your students:

- https://sproutsocial.com/insights/social-media-metrics-that-matter/.

As discussed throughout this book, from a business perspective, the purpose of social media is to drive revenue for your client. Different business models and objectives will benefit from different metrics. Some businesses may be interested in driving traffic from social media to a landing page. Other businesses may be interested in increased brand awareness. The important thing is for your students to understand how to gather and interpret this data and to see this data in terms of your client's business objectives.

This is significant because without a way to measure and show successful outcomes, one cannot make a business case for investing in social media. In

---

[23] For an in depth look at social media measurement and metrics, see Social Media Measurement and Management: Entrepreneurial Digital Analytics by Jeremy H. Lipschultz.

other words, if a company is spending money and resources on social media but they do not know if that is a profitable investment, then the company has no grounding for their decision. A decision without grounding is unstable and more easily reversible than a decision grounded on measurable data. Simply put, if your students want to work in social media, they need to be able to prove that their efforts are revenue-producing.

The typical marketing sales funnel argues that prospects can be moved from the top to the bottom of the funnel through some configuration of the following six steps: Awareness, consideration, preference, action, loyalty, and advocacy. A simpler way of thinking about this funnel is: Awareness, interest, and action. Building off of this, we can categorize the following metrics:

1. **Reach:** The number of people that may be aware of your message.
2. **Engagement:** The ways in which people interact with your message. This denotes some interest in your message.
3. **Acquisition:** A relationship is built – e.g., a lead is generated, a person subscribes to your email list or blog.
4. **Conversion:** Action is taken – usually, a sale.
5. **Loyalty & Advocacy:** The person buys again, tells someone else about your product, posts a positive review, etc.

At the end of the day, you want your students to be able to show how engagement is leading to acquisition, conversion, or other factors that drive revenue, such as loyalty and advocacy. However, that is often difficult to do in a classroom setting. Unless your client gives you access to Google Analytics, Facebook Ads Manager, HubSpot, or another platform that enables the tracking of users through a sales funnel, it may be challenging to demonstrate revenue generation within the confines of your class. However, by using free trackable URLs such as Bitly (https://bitly.com), you can show how different campaigns drive traffic to the client's website – which may or may not lead to influencing buying behavior or other desired outcomes. Bitly is a great tool because it shows the time, location, and source of a click on the URL. Thus, you are able to determine where your traffic is coming from.

Alternatively, tools like Instagram Insights show the number of actions taken via the profile, including clicks on the URL in the account profile (see Image 7 below).

If you do have access to your client's Google Analytics, and time permits, then you may find it helpful to teach your students to create social media campaigns by using UTM parameters. See this post on UTM parameters by Neil Patel:

- https://neilpatel.com/blog/the-ultimate-guide-to-using-utm-parameters/.

Custom UTM URLs can be built easily using the Google Analytics Campaign URL Builder:

- `https://ga-dev-tools.appspot.com/campaign-url-builder/`.

Actions Taken on Your Account

May 22, 2019 - May 28, 2019
4 Actions

May 22	May 23	May 24	May 25	May 26	May 27	May 28

0 Website Visits
▲ 0 from previous 7 days

4 Profile Visits
▲ 1 from previous 7 days

0 Calls
▲ 0 from previous 7 days

0 Texts
▲ 0 from previous 7 days

0 Emails
▲ 0 from previous 7 days

0 Get Direction
▲ 0 from previous 7 days

Image 7. Actions taken on the @ShepComm Instagram account during a weeklong period as shown on the Facebook Creator Studio. Note the low engagement during summer break, a time when we are not actively posting to the account.

While not perfect, it is possible to search for patterns between the desired revenue-generating behavior (e.g., someone buying a hat on the client's website) and the link clicks on your client's social media profile (e.g., Instagram as noted above) or the trackable URL your students are using in their social media content. For example, imagine that a Tweet promoting discounts on hats includes a trackable URL to a sales page. The trackable URL data shows that 10 Twitter users clicked on the link. Soon thereafter, your client's data shows that five hats were sold. While you cannot determine with certainty that your Tweet drove the sales, there is a likelihood that it contributed to those sales. However, other possible explanations need to be considered such as other ongoing promotions or daily sales trends.

While the confines of a social media class can make it difficult to show direct impact on the bottom line, there are many metrics you can teach your students which can have business value to your client and which may directly or indirectly impact revenue.

Before we get into those, let's review a few concepts relevant to the overall success of any campaign. It is critical that metrics are aligned with the client's campaign goals, objectives, target audience, and strategy. In addition to goals and objectives, two concepts your students should be familiar with are:

1. **Benchmarks:** A pre-campaign measurement. It is what you are measuring against. Such benchmarks allow you to track progress (Clampitt, 2018). An easy way to get students to understand this concept

is to use the analogy of exercise. Imagine you decide to start running to get in shape. On the first day you run a mile, your time is 8:15. That mile time is the benchmark against which you will measure the success of your future mile times.

2. **Key Performance Indicator (KPI):** The criteria for success in your campaign. This is also sometimes called a Key Progress Indicator (Kim, 2016). KPIs are tied to objectives. If an objective is to raise $10,000 in donations by September 15, then the KPI is $10,000. To turn to our exercise analogy, if the objective is to get your mile time down to 7:45 by race day on May 1, then your KPI is a mile time of 7:45.

Practitioners and scholars have categorized social media metrics in many ways. Quesenberry (2016) hones in on awareness, engagement, and customer service. Clampitt (2018) proposes four categories of social media metrics: Audience composition, traffic patterns, engagement metrics, and community sentiment. Further, social media metrics categories contain several metrics within them. For example, citing Kaushik (2011), Kim (2016) examines four community engagement metrics: Conversation rate, amplification rate, applause rate, and economic value.

Following the sales funnel above, I will focus on reach (awareness), engagement, and acquisition metrics on social media. I list many common metrics below. In discussing engagement metrics, I have categorized them using the classifications of applause, conversation, and amplification from Kim (2016) (see Kim, 2016, pp. 166-168). You will see many of these metrics on the Social Media Measurement spreadsheet discussed below. Note that each social media platform may define these terms differently and may or may not provide these metrics:

Reach (Awareness)

- **Followers:** Total number of followers at a given time.
- **Audience growth rate:** How much your audience grows or shrinks over a given time. Divide new audience members over total audience members. Example: If you add 10 new followers and have 100 followers, 10/100 = 10% growth rate.
- **Post reach (actual audience, impressions, views):** Number of accounts that your post was served up to. These are the people that, if they were paying attention, saw your post.
  - o **Video views:** Number of views of your video.
  - o **Story views:** Number of views on your story on Instagram Stories or Snapchat.
- **Potential audience:** The potential reach is the total number of people that could have possibly seen your post had they all been logged in and paying attention when your post was served up. This may be your follower count if no one shared or retweeted your post. If it was shared or retweeted,

then it also includes the followers of those people who shared/retweeted it.

- **CPM:** (only applicable when you are using paid social media) This is the cost per one thousand impressions.
- **Share of audience:** The percentage of persons reached by your client in comparison to its competitors. To calculate this, you would need to define the size of the audience. Is it the total number of followers you and your audience has? The total number of users that are posting with a particular hashtag? Operationalization of the audience will depend on the context.

Engagement

Monitoring community engagement with your client's audience is a way of staying abreast of how your online presence is interacting with your target audience and how your target audience is interacting with your client's online presence.

When we think of engagement, recall that there are low-threshold and high-threshold engagement metrics (see p. 124). The lower the threshold, the easier the action is to take and thus we can expect that more people will take them. Applause is a low-threshold engagement.

Applauses – Affinity, approval or emotional reaction to a post.

- **Likes / Favorites:** Number of likes or favorites on a post.
- **Reactions:** Emotional reactions on a post. Facebook uses: like, love, haha, wow, sad, angry. LinkedIn uses: celebrate, love, insightful, curious.
- **Screenshots:** Number of screenshots taken on a Snapchat story.
- **Sentiment:** The emotional response to your published content over a given time period. Usually categorized as: positive, negative, or neutral.
- **Applause rate:** The average number of likes or reactions a post gets.

Amplification – Shares or other actions that elevate the content to a wider audience.

- **Mentions:** Posts by other users that mention your client.
- **Check-ins:** When a user checks into your client's physical location on social media.
- **Shares:** Number of times your posts are shared by users.
- **Retweets:** Re-posts of your client's post by other users on Twitter.
- **Amplification rate:** The average amplification a post gets.

Conversation – The conversations occurring around a brand on social media.

- **Comments:** Number of comments per post.
- **Replies:** Replies to comments. This metric is used on some social platforms. For example, a reply on Facebook is a sub-comment to an existing comment in which a user mentions another user. In situations such as this, it is important that replies are not counted twice under both comments and replies.
- **Comment rate:** The average number of comments a post gets.

Additional engagement metrics include:

- **Engagement per follower:** The number of engagements divided by the number of followers. This metric is important for proving that followers are actually engaging with an account. Due to concerns of self-described influencers with many followers but little engagement[24], some brands are turning to this and similar metrics to evaluate the engagement a so-called influencer is getting.
- **Share of engagement:** The engagement of your client in comparison to its competitors.

<u>Acquisitions</u>

Here are but a few ways in which your social media efforts may drive acquisitions.

- **Clicks on Links:** Number of clicks on links shared on social media.
- **CPC (cost-per-click):** (only applicable when you are using paid social media) Average price paid for each click on a link in a paid post.
- **Blog subscribers:** Number of subscribers to a blog generated by social media.
- **Email subscribers:** Number of subscribers to an email list generated by social media.
- **Blog subscriber growth rate:** How much the number of blog subscribers grows or shrinks over a given time—which can be calculated by dividing new subscribers over total subscribers.
- **Email subscriber growth rate:** How much the number of email list subscribers grows or shrinks over a given time. You can calculate this rate by dividing new subscribers over total subscribers.
- **Leads:** Number of new leads generated from social media activity.
- **Traffic:** Number of visits and/or visitors to a website as generated by social media activity.

---

[24] See "An influencer with 2 million followers couldn't sell 36 t-shirts and Twitter is not okay" at:
https://www.msn.com/en-us/lifestyle/lifestyle-buzz/an-influencer-with-2-million-followers-couldnt-sell-36-t-shirts-and-twitter-is-not-okay/ar-AAC5hCs

A tour of the above concepts and tools via a brief lecture will help acquaint students with the importance of metrics.

How

Determine which metrics your students are going to track. As the professor, you can decide. Or, you can make this decision in a dialogue with your students.

Your students are going to use a spreadsheet to record and track metrics across several areas. This spreadsheet covers engagement metrics, social listening, and content optimization tracking. It is available in the chapter appendix and is titled the Social Media Measurement Spreadsheet. The spreadsheet is on Google Drive and each team will be able to make an editable copy of the spreadsheet that each team member can edit in real time on Google Drive. Thus, each team member will be able to participate in collecting and interpreting of the data for their social platform.

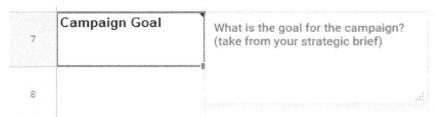

Image 8. Tips on the Social Media Measurement Spreadsheet can be found by scrolling over cells with small black triangles in the upper right. These will help your students complete the spreadsheet and save time.

I encourage you to load the Social Media Measurement Spreadsheet found in the chapter appendix before continuing with the rest of this chapter as I will be referring to it. Once you have it loaded, you will note that there are sheets (tabs) at the bottom of the spreadsheet. They are: Read Me, Planning, Metrics Goals, Reporting, Blog – Optimization Tracking, Instagram – Optimization Tracking, Twitter – Optimization Tracking, Snapchat – Optimization Tracking, and Social Listening. You will note that some cells have a small black triangle in the upper right-hand corner of the cell. If students place their computer mouse over these cells, a tip will appear (see the example in Image 8). The entire spreadsheet is editable. So you can modify it for your purposes and your students can do the same. Add and remove metrics, or entire sheets, per your needs.

Social media metrics can be gathered for free directly through each major social media platform. Twitter metrics can be gathered through Twitter Analytics (https://analytics.twitter.com).

Facebook page data can be viewed through Facebook Insights (learn more at https://www.facebook.com/help/search/?q=insights).

Instagram data can be gathered by viewing posts directly. As noted in Learning Objective 2 below, more advanced data can be gathered through Instagram Insights on the Instagram app or via a desktop computer through an Instagram Business (https://www.facebook.com/business/profiles) or Facebook Creator Studio account (http://facebook.com/creatorstudio).

Snapchat data can be seen in the Snapchat app. However, as I will discuss below, Snapchat data is very limited.

LinkedIn page data can be viewed through LinkedIn Page Analytics (https://www.linkedin.com/help/linkedin/answer/4499/linkedin-page-analytics-overview).

Web traffic data is dependent upon the content management system used for the page. The popular Wordpress content management system, which I use for our class blog, comes with its own basic analytics. However, Google Analytics (https://analytics.google.com/analytics/web) works with any website that allows for embedded code.

Alternatively, paid analytics dashboards will amalgamate your analytics for easy analysis and comparison.

If your class uses the HubSpot Academy, metrics on all social media content published through HubSpot can be analyzed through the HubSpot dashboard. See:

▪ https://knowledge.hubspot.com/articles/kcs_article/social/analyze-social-reports.

Do

It is time for student teams to work in class on setting up the Social Media Measurement Spreadsheet for the social media platform they are responsible for. For the present learning objective, your students will be working on 1) connecting their client's objectives with their metrics, 2) establishing their benchmarks and KPIs – that is, their metrics goals, and 3) reporting their metrics each week.

Reporting on metrics occurs each week following the week that students establish their benchmarks and KPIs. That is, each week the students will report on these metrics to look for changes in engagement with their social media content across time.

Because we want our students to think of metrics in context of the client's objectives, the first step is for students to try and link the client's objectives with the metrics they plan to track. This will be completed in the planning sheet on the spreadsheet. Give your students time in class to complete the planning sheet. They should pull the objectives from their strategic brief assignment (See how everything is interwoven?).

Have the student teams also work on their metrics goals in the metrics goals sheet. This is where teams establish what metrics they will track for the remainder of the semester. In the metrics goals sheet, also have the students determine the benchmark for that metric and the KPI, which they hope to achieve by the final week of the semester as that is the last week they will be tracking metrics. Recall, benchmarks and KPIs may include business metrics your client wants your students to track. Where applicable, a percentage increase between the benchmark and the KPI will be calculated. You will note that I have listed several social media platforms that can be tracked and their common metrics. But modify these or have your students modify them per the needs of the class. Go around the room and work with student teams as they complete the metrics goals sheet.

Once students have completed their planning and metrics goals sheets, reconvene the class so you can instruct them on the procedure for reporting on their metrics each week. Here is the procedure I recommend:

I give student teams 10 to 15 minutes at the start of class on the first day of the week that our class meets (e.g., Tuesday) to complete all the reporting, optimization, and social media listening sheets on the Social Media Measurement (we will discuss optimization and social media listening in learning objectives 2 and 3 below) . Students report the data for the previous seven days. For example, my class meets for the first time during a given week on Tuesdays. the data reported for the week 9 column consists of data for the previous seven days, meaning from Tuesday of week 8 to Tuesday of week 9. It is not the data from Sunday to Saturday during week 9, but rather the data for the previous week that is being collected during week 9.

I have found that giving students time in class means they are more likely to complete work. Some students shudder at anything that involves numbers. Afraid to ask for help, these students would simply not complete the tasks. Thus, I encourage you to give your students time at the start of each week to complete the spreadsheet for that week. During this time, go around the room and engage them, answer their questions, and help them get comfortable.

Because I begin teaching this material generally during week 8 of the semester, students begin to track data in the reporting sheet during week 9. Reporting on changes in social media engagement can be done in the reporting sheet of the Social Media Measurement Spreadsheet. Here is where you can also add revenue-related metrics or other business metrics your client wants you to track. Keep in mind that the metrics listed on the metrics goals sheet and the reporting sheet need to align. So, if any metrics are added, deleted, or modified in the metrics goals sheet, students will also need to make those same modifications to the reporting sheet.

In the reporting sheet, note that the %change column is a week-to-week change and not a cumulative change such that the %change for week 10 shows the %change for that metric when compared to week 9.

There is one caveat to all of this: Snapchat (Remember when I warned you about Snapchat back in Chapter 2?). Snapchat data is limited and quite frustrating to work with. Metrics on posts on Snapchat are only available for the duration of the post. Thus, the Snapchat group will have to complete this work outside of class. Unfortunately, sometimes students forget to collect this data. That is why I have sometimes found that the Snapchat team reports incomplete data on their content optimization. Unfortunately, at this time, detailed analytics are only available to highly-influential Snapchat accounts ("Insights," n.d.). In working with the Snapchat team, I have found it best to assign one student each week to be in charge of collecting Snapchat metrics.

Reflect

Reflection occurs in two ways. Students reflect on what they are learning as you go around the classroom and provide assistance. Ask them questions that will lead them to discover the answers, such as: Why might tracking comments on Instagram posts be useful to our client? Another opportunity for reflection comes during presentations. As you will see in the Content Period 2 assignment, students are required to turn in their up-to-date spreadsheet when turning in their other materials for the assignment. They are also required to discuss their metrics goals, benchmarks, KPIs, and data they have collected in the reporting tab during their presentation. I give teams a few minutes at the beginning of class on the day of presentations to collect their data for the week so that what they are presenting and turning in to me is up to date. If class time permits, you can also have class-wide discussions each week after student teams have reported their data, probing students for what trends they are seeing or how their progress is going towards their KPIs.

Learning Objective 2: Content Optimization

What and Why

Social media metrics can also be used to help you find out what works and what doesn't in terms of your social media content. Evaluating how your content is performing can help you answer questions such as: Which of your posts are getting the most engagement? What hashtags are getting the most engagement? Does your audience tend to engage with your content more when it is posted at certain times of day or days of the week? Do video posts earn more engagement than photo posts?

By stepping back and comparing how different pieces of social content are performing, your students can find out what works and do more of that. This will increase their chances of success with future content. This process is known as content optimization.

Anything that can be measured can be potentially evaluated to help increase the effectiveness of social media posts. Your students' ability to optimize their content is constricted only by the number of variables and the amount of data you want them to collect – that is, how many metrics you want them to consider. Common optimization variables one can assess include: Time of publication, date of publication, use of images or video, hashtags used, number of hashtags used, text length of a post, social media accounts tagged, and use of emojis.

Brands optimize content all the time. They're constantly monitoring what works and what doesn't and making tweaks. They do this not only with social media content, but with online ads, landing pages, email marketing, SEO and more.

Image 9. Reach and Impressions for an Instagram post as seen on Instagram Insights through the Instagram app.

How

Determine what content optimization variables you want your students to track. If you are not sure, you can have them track the common variables I have listed on the optimization tracking sheets in the social media measurement spreadsheet in the chapter appendix. You will note that I have created a different optimization tracking sheet for the different social media platforms we use in my class. That is because each platform provides slightly different engagement metrics. Also, those metrics can change over time so it is important to update the sheets as necessary.

For students to see what variables may increase the effectiveness of their posts, they will need to operationalize the term "effective." That is, how does the client define the effectiveness of a social media post? That goes back to campaign objectives. Is it the number of likes a post gets? Is it whether that post drives traffic to a landing page? Have a discussion with your students about what the desired outcome of their social media posts are. Likely, you've already had this conversation when they were working on their strategic briefs. But now is a good time for a reminder. Additionally, discuss what content optimization variables you are going to have them track.

Students will probably need to measure engagement with the post as engagement tends to indicate the effectiveness of a post. For engagement metrics, I have my students track potential audience and actual audience. I also have them track conversation rate – the rate of conversation on social (e.g., comments) - , amplification rate – behaviors that spread the content to a wider audience (e.g., retweets and shares) - , and applause rate – affinity for content (e.g., likes)(see Kim, 2016). (see the Social Media Measurement Spreadsheet in the chapter appendix). If you have access to revenue or other relevant business metrics for your client (e.g., web traffic, profile clicks, conversions), you can track them per post as well.

All of the metrics needed to complete the optimization sheets is available by looking at the posts and account information for each social media platform (sans revenue or business metrics, which will need to be provided by the client). No special software is needed. For example, if your students are tracking a post for Instagram, they can find all of optimization variable data by looking at the post itself – did it have hashtags, photo or video, etc.? Just about all of the audience and engagement metrics can be determined by analyzing the client's social media account and the post itself (having Instagram Insights will provide additional data and enable your students to determine the reach, or actual audience, for the post as well as where impressions are coming from: Home, hashtags, profile, or other. See Image 9).

Do

As a reminder, I am usually teaching this material during week 8 of the semester and thus students start tracking their optimized content during week 9 of the semester. As noted above, I give students about 10 to 15 minutes in class at the start of class on the first day of the week that our class meets (e.g., Tuesday) to complete their metrics reporting for the week. While students are collecting their data, remember to go around the classroom and offer guidance.

It is important to be mindful of a detrimental flaw in this approach to tracking for content optimization. If during one week, students enter the optimization data on Tuesday for a post that was published on the previous Friday and the next Tuesday they do the same for a post that was published the previous Wednesday, then an equal amount of time did not pass between their recording of data. The post published on Wednesday may have higher engagement just because more time passed between when it was published and when the metrics were recorded. I have found that although flawed, this approach is sufficient for the classroom setting in which students are learning these skills so long as I emphasize the flaws and teach my students the better approach for when they are out in the workplace. The better approach would be to have your students wait a consistent amount of time between when a post is published and when its data is recorded to have more comparable data from which you can glean more accurate insights. While this is ideal, I prefer to have my students recording metrics in class whenever possible.

For content optimization, I used to require my students to track data on each of the posts they published. However, I found this was an onerous task that was taking a great deal of time and getting in the way of other learning. Thus, I now require my students to track one post per week. I let them pick the post. This allows them to learn these skills in a manageable setting.

Reflect

There are two opportunities for reflection with this exercise. The first opportunity is to engage in discussion with your students about their findings as you go around the room while the students are recording their data at the start of class. The second opportunity is for students to offer their analysis and interpretation of the data they have collected during their Content Period 2 (and later, Content Period 3) presentations (see the Content Period 2 assignment in the appendix). In these presentations, student groups should be able to tell you how they are making changes to their content based on what they are seeing in their content optimization tracking.

Learning Objective 3: Ongoing Social Media Listening

In Learning Objective 1 of this chapter, I said that numbers matter. Qualitative measurements matter too. One does not matter more than the other. What matters is the combination of both qualitative and quantitative data as one informs the other. Ongoing social media listening is a great way for your students to practice their qualitative skills.

In Chapter 4, I discussed social media listening. Indeed, Unit 2 is dedicated to social media listening. So, I am not going to repeat the what and the why here. You may feel that your students need a refresher on what social media listening is and why we do it. If so, return to the material in Chapter 4, Learning Objective 1. If anything, a revisit to Boolean search skills will serve your students well here.

What your students are going to do now is set up and maintain weekly monitoring of the conversation surrounding your client and online conversations that are relevant to them. This weekly social media listening is part of the wider skillset your students are developing in this unit surrounding social media data collection and analysis.

How

If your class has access to use social media listening software such as Meltwater, then your students can use it to conduct their social media listening. You can also use social media dashboards like Hootsuite (discussed on pages 50-51) to do this social media listening. If not, your students can use free tools (see the list of software on page 48). Of the free tools, I like Social Searcher (https://www.social-searcher.com) for social media listening. Students can also go directly to the social media platform you want them to monitor.

Your students will use the social listening sheet on the Social Media Measurement Spreadsheet to complete their weekly social media listening (see the chapter appendix). There is a list of eight questions in column A of the social listening sheet. The questions are designed for students to both report and interpret data. Please modify them to your needs.

To help my students conduct their ongoing social listening, I create a lab guide that quickly teaches them how to set up and program the required searches to get the data they need (lab guides were discussed on page 53). This is a huge time saver for me because it prevents me from having to remind students each week how to gather their data. For example, when my students were using Meltwater, I provided them the following lab guide which showed them how to use Meltwater to answer each data-related question on the sheet:

- http://bit.ly/322_meltwaterlabguide.

Do

Just as is the case for the first two learning objectives in this chapter, students are given time at the start of the week each week to gather the data and enter it into their team's spreadsheet. Go around the classroom and assist the students.

Reflect

As above, reflection occurs in two ways: 1) while you go around the class, and 2) when they present their data to the class during their presentations.

While assisting students as they collect their data, challenge them to think critically. Why are they interpreting the data the way they are? There is a question in the social listening sheet that reads: "In your opinion, what is the most important takeaway from this week?" Further, ask your students: What actions can I take with this data?

Recommended Readings

Analyze social reports (2019, May 3). *HubSpot Academy*. Retrieved from https://knowledge.hubspot.com/articles/kcs_article/social/analyze-social-reports

Bonner, M. (2019, May 29). An influencer with 2 million followers couldn't sell 36 t-shirts and Twitter is not okay. Cosmopolitan. Retrieved from https://www.msn.com/en-us/lifestyle/lifestyle-buzz/an-influencer-with-2-million-followers-couldnt-sell-36-t-shirts-and-twitter-is-not-okay/ar-AAC5hCs

Jackson, D. (2018, April 2). All of the social media metrics that matter. Sprout Social. Retrieved from https://sproutsocial.com/insights/social-media-metrics-that-matter

Lipschultz, J.H. (2019). Social Media Measurement and Management: Entrepreneurial Digital Analytics. New York, NY: Routledge.

Patel, N. (n.d.). The ultimate guide to using UTM parameters. Neil Patel. Retrieved from https://neilpatel.com/blog/the-ultimate-guide-to-using-utm-parameters

Chapter 7 Appendix

Content Period 2 Assignment

Note to the reader: Provide the Social Media Brand Guidelines to your students (see the Chapter 5 Appendix). These are the same guidelines they should have used in creating their strategic briefs. Recall that the Social Media Grading Rubric can be distributed to students to guide them in creating their content. In fact, I attach it to the bottom of the assignment when I distribute the assignment to my students. You can use it to assist in grading (see the Chapter 5 Appendix).

In the below assignment, modify the time period for which you want the students creating proposed content based on your needs.

The instructions tell the students to organize their content using the content calendar the professor will provide. This is a reference to the Social Media Content Calendar Template referenced in the Chapter 5 Appendix. Make a shareable copy with your students with updated dates to reflect the weeks for which your students will be creating content.

The referenced Social Media Measurement spreadsheet is available in the Chapter 7 Appendix below.

Lastly, recall the list of resources provided in Chapter 5 which may help students in designing their social media content (see p. 87).

Overview

Purpose
For Content Period 2, your team will create **1 batch** (see definition below) of content which can be spread out over a 5-week period during the 11th, 12th, 13th, 14th and 15th week of the semester.

To Do
1. Relying on your strategic brief, the monitoring you've done of your social media channel, and any feedback you received regarding your Content Period 1 content:
    a. Create content for your social channel for the assigned weeks. Consider any dates, events, or other tie-ins on the calendar for that time frame (e.g., Thanksgiving, Fall break, etc.).
2. In creating this content, plan to use at least 1 of the influencers your team identified in Content Period 1. Explain your plan in your presentation.

a. Are you going to ask this person to be featured in your content? Are you hoping to mention them in a piece? Are you going to ask them to please share our content? etc.

3. Track key metrics each week in the Social Media Measurement spreadsheet I have provided.

Content Tasks

You have 3 tasks:

1. Content Requirements (Quality > quantity)

Organized for the time period assigned in the form of the social media content calendar, my primary concerns are:

- Each piece of content ties together – it is purposive and fits with the plan you created in your strategic brief assignment.
- You've created audience centric, original content that will stand out.
- It's of a high professional quality (writing, editing, visuals, etc.).

Content Period 2 Batch =

- Blogs: 4 posts spread across the 5 weeks – About ¾ to 1-page double spaced text. Minimum of 2 visuals per post needed.
  - For each post you need to provide 2 different promotional tweets. Write these in the content calendar on the day that you want your blog to be published and the day after.
- Instagram, Twitter, Snapchat: 10 posts of ORIGINAL visuals and text

2. Track Metrics

Your team will track key metrics for your social channel.

Turn in the latest version when submitting your assignment materials.

How? Download a copy in .XLS format and submit it with your other materials.

You'll be responsible for filling out the data each week. This will be turned in for this project, but also at the end of the semester when all data has been entered.

Grading Criteria

- Appropriateness of work to the situation, audience, and client
- Professional quality of content
- Extent to which content is consistent with project goals
- Extent to which content is consistent with team's strategy as put forth in their strategic brief
- Considers/adapts to feedback given by professor

Presentation Tasks

Your group will present your content to the class.
Time: About 8 minutes of presentation time.

Be sure to address:
1. Content:
   - How your content fits with your content categories (i.e., your 'content buckets').
   - How your content takes into consideration the monitoring you've done of your social media channel, and any feedback you received via your Content Period 1.
   - Discuss how your influencer(s) are being integrated into your content plan and how that aligns with your strategic brief and/or content goals.
2. Metrics:
   - Explain what metrics you plan to track, and your benchmark, and your final week goals (KPIs).
   - Go over the metrics you have tracked so far.
   - In terms of optimization: What variables (e.g., hashtags, photo versus video, etc.) are associated with posts that are getting higher engagement?
   - Analyzing and interpreting all the data you tracked, answer: What actions could your client take with this knowledge?

Q&A / Evaluation
Afterwards, your classmates (who are roleplaying as the client) will evaluate your presentation and will be encouraged to ask you questions.

Expectations
This is a casual presentation. Not all members have to speak, but they must be present in class on that day and join the team at the podium or they will receive -10% of the group's grade.

Social Media Measurement Spreadsheet

Note to the reader: Access the Social Media Measurement spreadsheet via the URL below. You can download the spreadsheet for your own use or save a copy to your Google Drive folder. To save it to your Google Drive, sign into Google. Then, click "File" -> "Make a Copy" and follow the instructions. I encourage you to make a second copy and use that copy to share with your students. That way, you'll have the original file just in case. You can make the file shareable to your student teammates by clicking the "Share" button in the upper right hand corner of the spreadsheet. Simply share the URL that Google generates with your students. Then, have someone in each student group make a copy and save it to their Google account. That student will then share the file to their team, choose the option to let anyone with the link edit the file. This will allow each team to edit the spreadsheet and thus every team member can work on the file simultaneously.

Full URL:

https://docs.google.com/spreadsheets/d/1osGpqUa2Dw6sP8ME4N-Ck6BAtqLinuau3_B5mx-_0dg/edit?usp=sharing

Short Link (case sensitive):

http://bit.ly/2I9rFvB

CHAPTER 8: UNIT 6. CONTENT PERIOD 3 AND PAID SOCIAL MEDIA ADVERTISING

In the final unit, students learn about social media advertising. They learn how Facebook Business tools are used to plan, create, and execute paid social media. Students complete the Content Period 3 assignment, their final content assignment for the class client. Students deliver a final presentation.

Content periods 1 and 2 focused on helping students learn to plan, create, and execute social media content for a client. Yet, anyone who has followed social media trends knows that organic reach has fallen precipitously in the last few years (Erskine, 2018). As social media companies like Facebook and Twitter have gone from venture backed to publicly traded, they need to show financial growth to shareholders. These companies generate revenue through targeted advertising. However, Facebook states on its website that profit is not a factor in the decline of organic reach (Boland, 2014). Instead, Facebook cite two reasons: 1) The growing amount of content being posted to Facebook and, 2) The company's goal of tweaking News Feed to show only the most relevant content to each individual user (Boland, 2014).

Whatever the reason, organic reach on Facebook is a shadow of what it was just a few years ago. Some sources claim that Facebook's organic reach has fallen to as low as 2% while others cite a slightly higher 6.4% (Bain, 2019; Butler, 2017; Erskine, 2018; Zelm, 2018).

The lesson is clear. Paid social media must be a part of an effective social media strategy. It is no longer enough to create compelling content, publish it on social media, and expect to reach one's target audience. So now that our students have learned how to strategize, plan social media content, identify and work with influencers, track social metrics and conduct social listening, we must teach them to integrate these skills on the paid side. Once students have learned this preceding material, an understanding of paid social media as a vehicle for targeting audiences and delivering content can be added and more easily executed. However, you may decide that it works best for your class to cover paid social media earlier in the semester.

In this chapter, you will teach students about paid social media advertising and the role it plays in an effective social media strategy. You will teach your students about the Facebook Ads Manager. You will get your students creating ads with specific audiences in mind.

I highly recommend completing the Facebook Blueprint courses discussed in this chapter and acquainting yourself with Facebook Ads

Manager and the Facebook Creative Hub before teaching this material to your students.

Suggested Schedule: Weeks 11, 12, 13, 14 and 15

1. Day 21: What is paid social media advertising and how does it work?; Introduce Facebook Advertising Case Study Presentation Assignment (optional)
2. Day 22: Facebook Advertising Case Study Presentation Assignment Lab Time (optional). Note: This time can otherwise be used as lab time for Content 3 or for lab time to work on learning Facebook Ads Manager and the related activities.
3. Day 23: Objective-oriented, targeting advertising campaigns; Create a Campaign and Ad Set in the Facebook Ads Manager Activity
4. Day 24: Ad Creative; Create a Social Media Advertisement in the Facebook Creative Hub Activity
5. Day 25: Thanksgiving Break
6. Day 26: Thanksgiving Break
7. Day 27: Introduce campaign reporting and the use of data to improve advertising success; Facebook Campaign Reporting and Data Knowledge Check Activity
8. Day 28: Catch up time as needed; Content 3 work day
9. Day 29: Content 3 work day
10. Day 30: Content 3 presentations. Note: If you want to give your students more time to work on Unit 6, have their Content Period 3 presentations due during finals week and adjust the weeks that you have assigned your students to create content for back one week so that it does not include finals week.

Unit Learning Objectives

1. Introduce students to paid social media advertising.
2. Teach students the skills to plan objective-oriented, targeted advertising campaigns.
3. Teach students to use analytical and problem solving abilities to follow the objective-oriented, targeted approach to creating social media ads.
4. Introduce students to the use of campaign reporting and data to improve advertising success. Have them apply critical thinking to the interpretation of data.

Content Period 3 Assignment

The Content Period 3 Assignment is available in the chapter appendix. Go over the assignment with your students. Recall that the teams will be required to present their content to the class. This will be their last presentation and you should expect a deeper reflection from your students on their work over the course of the semester. There is a presentation evaluation sheet in the Chapter 6 appendix which you can have your students complete to provide feedback to one another.

I do not expect that your class, or more accurately the client you are working for, has a budget to allow your students to create and publish paid advertising. Further, each team in your class is in charge of a different social media platform and thus paid social media advertising may not be available to each team. Thus, I did not include a requirement for students to create paid social media ads as part of the Content Period 3 assignment. However, I encourage you to add paid social media content as a requirement if it fits into the affordances of your class. This would, of course, be ideal because your students will get to see the metrics for their paid social advertising and learn from what works and what doesn't. But, don't worry if it's not a possibility. There are a few options to expose your students to these skills.

The What, Why, How, Do, Reflect

Learning Objective 1: Basics of How Paid Social Media Advertising Works

What

Ad Bidding

Social media advertising has enabled everyone from the solopreneurs to the multi-national company to pay to target specific audiences on social media platforms with easy-to-use tools. Because users can set their own budget of just a few dollars, an entity with a small budget has access to the same tools that entities with big budgets have.

While each social media platform has its own tools and processes for reaching target audiences, social media advertising works broadly on a bidding system, or advertising auction system. This works similarly to the auction systems that Google and Bing use to deliver up search engine advertisements.

Your students need to understand the bidding system of advertising auctions because several inputs dictate whether or not their advertisement or their competitor's advertisement gets displayed to the target audience. A brief lecture will be instructive to helping students get these new and sometimes confusing concepts. Note that while there are other ways to buy social media advertising, this lecture will focus on advertising auctions as they are the most common form of purchasing ads on social media that your students will experience.

The idea of the auction system is that several organizations might be competing to have their advertising displayed to members of a target audience. Because the target audience's attention is limited, only one ad will be displayed. Think of it like a billboard. You only drive by it once in a car ride. If there is only one billboard, then there is only one chance for you to see an ad. Although several organizations might like to advertise on that billboard, only one can. The same idea works on a social media news feed. The instance where the ad will be displayed passes by as a user scrolls. But in social media advertising, many organizations might be competing to have their ad be the one ad the user sees. How do they do that? They bid on the ad space and the 'best ad' wins.

So what makes an ad the 'best ad'?

For purposes of demonstration, we will focus on Facebook because it is the largest social media platform in the world. The ad auction process Facebook uses extends to Instagram, Facebook Messenger and the Facebook Audience Network.

Facebook cares about a few factors when choosing which ad to display: 1) The advertiser's bid – or, how much money the person is willing to pay for the ad space, the 2) Estimated Action Rates, and 3) The User Value. The formula Facebook uses to determine the total value of an advertisement is ("Ad Auction and Delivery Overview, 2019):

Total Value = [Advertiser Bid] X [Estimated Action Rates] + [User Value]

Estimated action rates are behaviors like engagements or conversions and are defined as "the probability that showing an ad to a person leads to [the] desired outcome of the advertiser" ("About ad auctions, n.d., ¶ 10). In other words, Facebook ads are optimized to users based on their past behavior.

The User Value factors in the relevance of the ad to the target audience and the ad quality ("Ad Auction and Delivery Overview," 2019). Ad quality is a measure derived from many inputs including user feedback such as hiding or reporting ads, after click behavior, and more ("About ad auctions, n.d.). Taken together, higher user value can lower the cost to achieve the desired objective for advertisers. Alternatively, lower user value can make an ad cost more to display.

There are several different actions, or objectives, an advertisement on Facebook can have. But broadly speaking, there are three: 1) Awareness, 2) Consideration, and 3) Conversion ("About advertising objectives," n.d.). When an advertiser creates an ad, the advertiser chooses a desired objective, such as brand awareness. That desired objective will influence how the ad is displayed. If an advertiser is seeking clicks on an ad, then the estimated action will be optimized for the likelihood that the target audience will click on the advertisement[25].

Once an advertisement has received 500 impressions, Facebook begins to provide metrics on the relevance of the ad. As of April 30, 2019, three factors determine the relevance of an advertisement (Gesenhues, 2019a): 1) Quality ranking – or perceived quality when compared to competing ads, 2) Engagement rate ranking – or, the expected engagement rate as compared with competing ads, and 3) Conversion rate ranking – or, the expected conversion rate as compared to competing ads ("About ad auctions," n.d.). You can learn more about how ad relevance diagnostics can help advertisers improve their ads:

- https://www.facebook.com/business/help/436113280262012?helpref=faq_c ontent.

Budgeting

When creating an advertisement campaign, advertisers set a budget. They also set the duration for which the campaign will run. By default, Facebook displays advertisements evenly throughout a campaign duration ("Ad Auction and Delivery Overview, 2019). While bidding strategies are beyond the scope of this book[26], it is important for students to understand the basics of advertising budgeting. There are two types of budgets for individual Facebook ads:

1. **Total budget (Lifetime Budget):** The max spend on an ad before the ad stops running. Example: A total budget of $50 means you will spend up to $50 on the ad.
2. **Daily budget:** The max daily average spend on an ad. Example: A $10 daily budget set to run over seven days would cost you up to $70.

The duration of days that the advertisement will run is an important factor in the total spend on the ad.

Often, an organization will be running more than one advertisement at a time. For example, Facebook advertisement campaigns can be created which allow you to create a group of ads with a common objective. Thus, a spending limit can be set across all ads that are running so that the total spending across all ads does not exceed the limit.

Determining an advertising budget is more complicated than simply

---

[25] Regardless of the objective chosen, all ads compete on equal footing in the bidding process because Facebook converts all bids to an eCPM, or effective cost per 1,000 impressions. Think of it like a Z-score. It allows different objective types to be compared in kind. Learn more at: https://www.linkedin.com/pulse/facebook-ecpm-first-only-thing-you-need-know-dario-di-feliciantonio.

[26] You can learn about bid strategies here: https://www.facebook.com/business/help/1619591734742116

picking a daily or total budget. The value produced from the advertisement must be taken into consideration along with the cost of advertising. As you will see below, other costs a business incurs must also be taken into consideration.

First, you may find it helpful to teach or refresh your students on return on investment or ROI. ROI is generally calculated:

ROI = (Money Received – Money Spent) / Money Spent

For example, imagine $1,000 is spent on Facebook ads over a one month period. That ad spending generated $1,500 in sales. So, the ad spending brought in $500 in profits. Then, we calculate ROI as:

ROI = (1,500 – 1,000) / 1,000 = 50%.

But while an ROI of 50% sounds great on paper, it does not tell us whether an ROI of 50% is a profitable return on investment, once the cost of business is factored in. This can be explained with another simple example. It is not profitable to spend $100 on paid social media ads to sell one widget (i.e., a cost-per acquisition of $100) with a profit margin of $50. Would you be willing to lose $50 every time you sold a product?

Questions of cost, such as production costs, shipping costs, and other costs, need to be taken into consideration when determining advertising budgets. For example, if the client sells coffee and it costs $.50 to make a cup of coffee and the coffee sells for $2, then a profit margin of $1.50 is working for the client's business. But, let's imagine the client only sells 10 cups a day for a daily profit of $15. To grow the client's business, the client needs more customers. The client may be willing to spend $.50 for each additional sale above the daily 10 cups sold. This will lower profit per additional cup of coffee sold to $1 ($.50 to make the coffee and $.50 to acquire the sale). However, if the client can sell 20 cups of coffee a day instead of 10, daily profits will grow. The new daily profit will be $25. This is calculated by adding up the client's usual $1.50 per cup profit on the first 10 cups sold, or $15 in profit, and $1 per cup profit on the additional 10 cups sold, or $10. As such, the $.50 cost per acquisition (CPA) is justified even though it will reduce the profit per cup.

Yet, this example fails to consider what it costs for the time spent creating and running the social media ads, including employee labor and materials. As you can see, it can be difficult to determine precise social media ROI.

If your class is working with an external client, you will need to align your class campaign objectives with the advertising objectives of the client. Pose questions about advertising objectives and budgeting to the client, or have your students pose them. Even if your class will not be spending actual money on behalf of the client, it is still a great learning experience for your students. Questions may include: What is the business value of the desired advertisement objective? How much is the client willing to spend to acquire a customer? To reach an audience? To drive X number of people to their website? For example, is the client willing to pay $10 to reach 2,000 people? If so, why? If not, why not? The client should have an understanding of its profit margin, how much it is willing to cut into it to grow its business, and what its profit margin needs to be to viably run its business.

Keep in mind that some business objectives may be more challenging to evaluate simply through metrics like views and engagements. Important business objectives such as reputation, awareness, and trust are more difficult to measure and may require additional research such as surveys or focus groups.

If your class is working with a smaller organization and advertising is new to them, then they may not know what the business value of advertising is. Your students may hear something like, "Let's just spend $100 and see if it does anything." In this case, you still need to know what the client's business objective for the campaign is (i.e., what they mean when they say 'if anything happens'). It may be advisable to start with a small budget of $5 to $10 a week, monitor ad metrics, and tweak from there.

If your class will not be doing any advertising on behalf of the client, then it is still worthwhile to have this conversation with your students as a hypothetical case for learning purposes.

Why

The Why is simple. As discussed above, organic reach on social media is down, particularly on Facebook properties. The need for employees with the skills to plan and execute paid social media, however, is up.

How

The best way to teach your students about how social media advertising works is to assign them to complete courses in Facebook Blueprint (https://www.facebook.com/business/learn). Facebook Blueprint is the set of courses and learning materials for digital marketing on Facebook properties. Facebook Blueprint offers basic courses, designed to provide quick and easy-to-learn skills for advertising on Facebook and Instagram. The program also offers an array of in depth professional courses for advanced learning (https://www.facebookblueprint.com/student/catalog). All of these classes are free, although a certification in Facebook Blueprint is possible but currently costs $300.

If you want your students to learn the basics, utilize the beginner's courses. If you want your students gain more advanced knowledge, select the professional courses that are right for you[27]. In an ideal world, students would complete all of the professional courses. But, there is only so much time in the day. So, I have my students complete the following professional courses:

- Get Started with Advertising
- Target the Right Audience
- Measure Ad performance
- One other course of their choosing from the following list: "Build awareness," "Drive consideration," "Generate leads," "Promote my app," "Manage ads," "Increase online sales."

I've also provided an optional Facebook Advertising Case Study Presentation assignment in the chapter appendix. This assignment allows your students to explore successful Facebook ads on the Facebook Creative Hub Gallery (https://www.facebook.com/ads/creativehub/gallery/) as well as work with the Facebook Audience Insights tool (discussed on p. 55 of the printed text). This assignment is great for helping students analyze high-quality social media advertisements while challenging them to deconstruct how a social media marketer thinks. This assignment can be done as an in-class presentation, as a video presentation turned in directly to the professor, or as a written assignment.

Do

Facebook Blueprint can be completed at home. The Facebook Advertising Case Study assignment can be worked on during class time or outside of class.

Reflect

Discuss with your students what their 'aha moments' were from Facebook Blueprint. Ask them what the 'muddiest,' or most confusing, points were from the coursework and generate a discussion aimed at empowering the students to help teach one another. Ask them how they could use what they learned to create an advertisement today to promote a sparkling water brand, an automobile, or a new video game.

If your students completed the Facebook Advertising Case Study assignment, use their presentations as a launching point for a discussion about the pros and cons of the advertisements they examined. Challenge

---

[27] Students can also learn how to create ads on other social media sites such as Twitter. However, in my opinion, if your students can run ads on Facebook, then they can work with Twitter. However, Twitter Flight School (https://flightschool.twitter.com) and Twitter for Business (https://business.twitter.com/en.html) are available resources.

them on their chosen target audience, per the questions in part three of the assignment.

Learning Objective 2: Objective-oriented, Targeted Advertising Campaigns
How to Build Ads: The Options

Once students have a grasp on social media advertising and an understanding of how the bidding and budgeting aspects of paid social media advertising work, it is time to teach them how to begin building social ads. Before designing ads, they need to learn how to set their ads up for success by determining advertising objectives and formats, choosing where their ad will run, and building a target audience.

When it comes to Facebook, advertisements can be created directly from a Facebook Page or through an Instagram Business account. They can also be built in the Facebook Ads Manager (https://www.facebook.com/business/tools/ads-manager).

Creating ads through a Facebook Page or Instagram Business account is a quick and simple process. It is a process designed to be doable by the widest possible user base. For example, it is here that existing Facebook or Instagram posts can be 'boosted,' or promoted to reach a wider audience. Indeed, Facebook Pages and Instagram Business accounts are the primary focus of the basic educational courses provided in Facebook Blueprint. In addition, when creating an ad this way, a step-by-step guide will walk your students through the required components of the advertisement, including objective, ad creative, target audience, and budget. The downside, however, is that your students will need access to a Facebook Page or Instagram Business account.

Alternatively, Facebook Ads Manger is part of the Facebook Business tools suite and is accessible to everyone with a Facebook account. Thus, we will focus on the Facebook Ads Manager in this book. It lets you set up Facebook campaigns that can target audiences across Facebook, Instagram, Facebook Messenger, and the Facebook Advertising Network.

Facebook advertisement campaigns are the organizing structure used to contain a series of advertisements under one advertising objective, such as reach. Next, there are ad sets. Ad sets are groups of ads within a campaign. Each ad set typically has a different audience. This way, messages can be tailored to different audiences. Different budgets can be set for different ad sets. Also, an ad set can target audiences on Facebook, Instagram, or the Facebook Advertising Network. Lastly, there are the ads themselves. The ads are the individual advertisements. For example, you may have a campaign with an objective to drive traffic to a website. The campaign has three ad sets. Ad set one targets doctors, ad set two targets patients, and ad set three targets health insurance companies. With each ad set, there are multiple ads. This allows you to see the effectiveness of different ad creative on driving traffic to your website for your different target audiences (see Image 10).

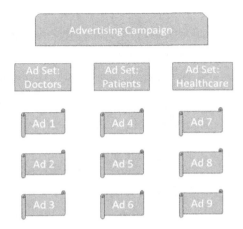

Image 10. Facebook advertising campaign flow chart.

The steps to creating and running a Facebook ad are ("Facebook ads: Reach out to future customers and fans," n.d.):

1. Choose the objective.
2. Select the audience.
3. Choose where the ad will run.
4. Set a budget.
5. Pick an ad format.
6. Place the order.
7. Monitor and manage the ad.

For now, your students need to understand ad objectives, ad formats, audience targeting, and ad placement. We have already discussed budget in Learning Objective 1.

Advertising Objectives and Ad Formats

When discussing budgets in Learning Objective 1, you should have discussed with your students what the client hopes to accomplish with paid social media. Does the client want to reach more people? Does the client want to drive traffic to a website? The advertisement objective should be derived from the campaign objectives for your class, which should be derived from your client's business objectives. Social media advertising is not separate from the social media strategic plan. It is part of the plan. It should be woven into the fabric of the client's goals and objectives as one of the tactics to execute a strategy. For example, if the strategy of one of your student teams is aimed at increasing awareness of events at a local coffee shop, paid social media can be used as a tactic to promote one of the events.

As noted above, advertising objectives are organized under three broad objectives: Awareness, consideration, and conversion. They are organized as follows ("Facebook ads objectives: Choose a marketing goal for your ads," n.d.):

- Awareness Objectives – for getting attention.
    - Brand Awareness
    - Reach
- Consideration Objectives – for engaging the audience.
    - App installs
    - Traffic
    - Lead generation
    - Messages
    - Engagement
    - Video views
- Conversion Objectives – for encouraging actions.
    - Conversions
    - Store visits
    - Catalog sales

Different ad formats were designed to work with different ad objectives. Once an objective is selected[28], Facebook offers the user the ad formats that were designed for that objective, making it easy to choose an appropriate format. You can learn more about these objectives here:

- https://www.facebook.com/business/ads/ad-objectives#.

A great resource to share with your students about each ad format, including specifications and reasons for using each ad format, is available here:

- https://www.facebook.com/business/ads-guide.

While your students will likely not recall all of the objectives, it is helpful to expose them to the list and then focus in on teaching them about the objectives that are relevant to your client.

Targeting the Right Audience

If your students worked with Facebook Audience Insights in any of the assignments discussed previously in this book, then they will have a leg up on how to research and identify the target audience for their ad.

---

[28] Recall that when building an advertisement in the Facebook Ads Manager, the objective is chosen at the campaign level.

Ad targeting can be done through the following variables:

- Location
- Age
- Gender
- Languages
- Detailed targeting – include/exclude based on demographics, interests, and behaviors.
- Connections – include/exclude persons based on connections to Facebook pages, apps, or events.

Once an audience is created, it can be saved for later use in new ads. In addition, custom audiences can be built by importing data collected through Facebook pixel (discussed later in this chapter), the Facebook SDK, and via engagement on Facebook.

To help elaborate on these concepts, I recommend showing the videos in class from the brief Facebook Blueprint course "Find Your People on Facebook":

- https://www.facebook.com/business/learn/lessons/facebook-ad-audience-considerations#.

After introducing these audience targeting variables, have a conversation with your students as to what variables they think would be relevant to ads that your client would run on social media. Some, such as location, may be more obvious than others. Show students some of the detailed audience categories and subcategories in Facebook Ad Manager (see Image 11 below). Have your students discuss which categories and subcategories may relate to your client. Better yet, have your students log into Facebook Ad Manager, start the ad set up process, and explore the categories and subcategories under the detailed targeting option.

Note that as you adjust the audience variables, the estimated daily results for the ad changes in real time (see Image 12 below). The better an advertiser knows the audience, the more targeted the advertiser can get, which will avoid wasted ad dollars. However, defining an audience too narrowly may result in too little ad reach. These estimates help you make some predictions as to how the ad will perform. This estimate is also affected by the budget for the ad. Bring your students' attention to these estimates and show them how they change.

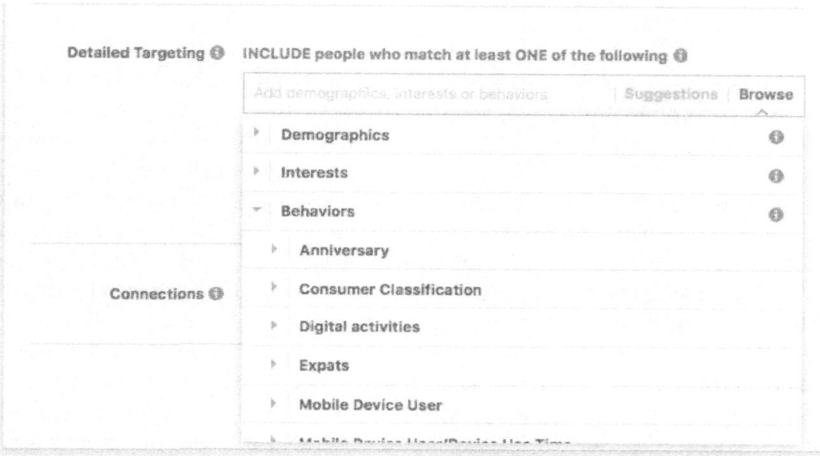

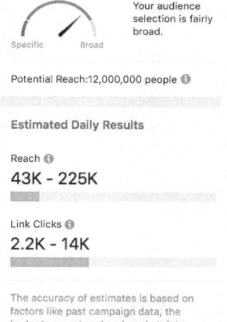

Image 11. Detailed targeting options as seen the Facebook Ads Manager.

Your audience selection is fairly broad.

Specific   Broad

Potential Reach:12,000,000 people ⓘ

Estimated Daily Results

Reach ⓘ
43K - 225K

Link Clicks ⓘ
2.2K - 14K

The accuracy of estimates is based on factors like past campaign data, the budget you entered and market data. Numbers are provided to give you an idea of performance for your budget, but are only estimates and don't guarantee results.

Image 12. Estimated Daily Results for an ad as seen the Facebook Ads Manager.

Ad Placement

As explained earlier, Facebook Ads Manager allows advertisers to choose on what Facebook properties their ad will run. The default is automatic placement, which distributes an ad across the Facebook properties. Automatic placement takes into consideration bid prices and thus maximizing budget. Alternatively, an advertiser can choose ad placements across feeds, stories, in-stream videos, messages, and contextual spaces. Ads can also be placed on apps and websites through the Facebook Audience Network, which is an advertising distribution network with reach outside of Facebook ("Audience network: Create an ad on Facebook. Show it across the Web," n.d.). Further, the advertiser can choose to have the ad shown on desktop, mobile, or both and can choose to have the ad shown on mobile devices only when the audience is on WIFI. This can beneficial when advertising with video, especially in areas where mobile connectivity is slow.

Choosing whether to use automated placement or manual selection of placement should be derived from a consideration of the ad objective, the target audience, and any other relevant context. There may be reasons to want ads to run only on certain properties. For example, if a business is primarily on Instagram and it is running a promotion for existing customers, then wider distribution would not be an effective use of budget. Further, if the ad is going to be a fun, quirky video, then promoting it on Instagram Stories rather than Instagram Feed may be a better fit. If a business relies heavily on Facebook and wants an offer to have an intimate feel, sponsored messages on Facebook Messenger may work as they only go to people who are already connected to an advertiser's business on Facebook. If widespread awareness is the goal, then an advertiser may opt for broad reach across the web through the Facebook Advertising Network.

Why

The why is the same as for Learning Objective 1.

How

Your students will apply what they are learning by completing the Create a Campaign and Ad Set in the Facebook Ads Manager Activity, which is available in the chapter appendix. For now, they are not going to come up with the ad creative. They are just going to define an advertising objective, pick an ad format, build a targeted audience, and choose the ad placement.

Working with Facebook Ads Manager for the first time can be overwhelming. You may want to offer some parameters to limit students' choices. You can do this by providing students with the advertising objective and explaining how that objective ties to the client's goals and objectives and how it might fit into each team's strategic plan. For example, try a reach or traffic objective. Next, you can also instruct students which ad format to use based on the objective chosen. The single image or video ad is a great format to learn on because it is simple and can be created with a single image or photo. You can also instruct students to use automatic placements or provide a budget. Lastly, you can offer some tips to help students hone in on their target audience. If you want to challenge your students a bit more or have a bit more time for your students to work on this, do not provide any of these parameters. In the assignment, I have provided all of the steps for students to practice. Modify the assignment to your needs.

Do

To complete this activity, the students will need to log into Facebook Ads Manager with their Facebook account. Your students may want to have Facebook Blueprint lesson "Create Facebook Ads" loaded for assistance when working on this activity. "Create Facebook Ads" is part of the "Get Started with Advertising" course. I encourage you to allow students to work on this activity in class so that you can offer guidance.

Reflect

The students write a brief reflection as part of the Create a Campaign and Ad Set in the Facebook Ads Manager Activity. But, talking with students about their choices in this assignment is a vital component of the learning process. After all, this is new to them and their confidence may be low. While perhaps the only real way to know if the students' choices were good would be to create and publish the ads and see how they performed, a lot of progress can be made by asking students to think about and justify their choices. Challenge their assumptions in a supportive environment. By allowing students to share the different choices they made, the students will learn from one another.

In truth, practice – ideally, with real data for feedback - is the only way to iterate and improve. So feel free to repeat this activity for multiple ad objectives and/or audiences relevant to your client.

Learning Objective 3: Ad Creative

What

Once students understand the advertisement parameters used to create an objective-oriented targeted advertisement, they are ready to build their own ads. In this section they are going to start building their own paid social media ad creative, thus completing their paid social ads.

In terms of ad creative, each social media platform has its own dimensions and requirements. For simplicity, we will focus on ad creative for Facebook properties.

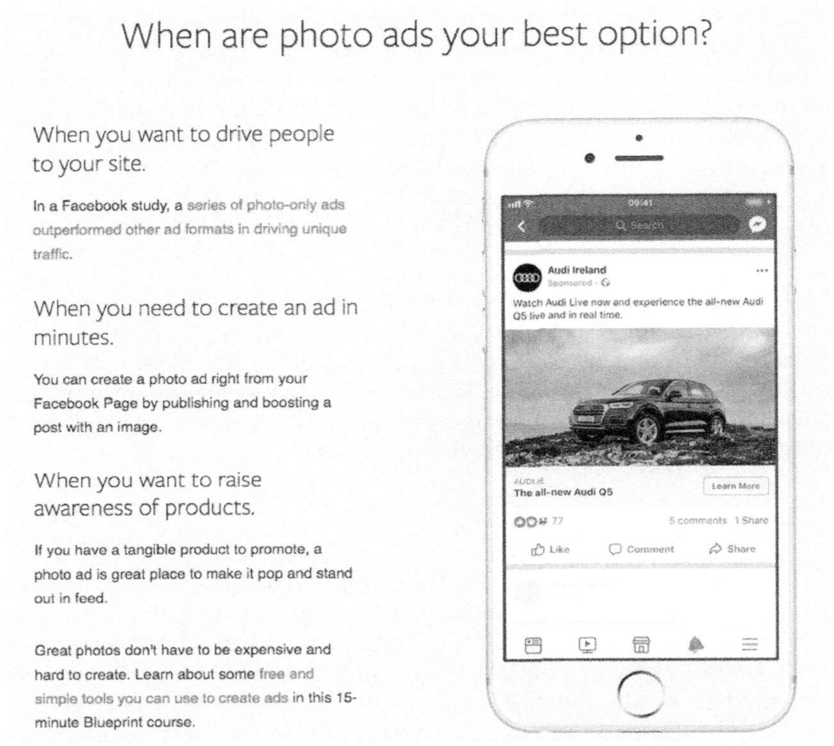

Image 13. Photo Ads webpage https://www.facebook.com/business/ads/photo-ad-format.

Students should be aware of the different ad formats that can be used to create an advertisement and what objectives they correspond with.

The best way to teach this is to review the up-to-date offerings on the Facebook ad formats page (https://www.facebook.com/business/ads-guide) (also discussed above) with your students. This is a great resource for familiarizing your students with the possible ad formats that they can use when creating an ad. For specific examples alongside explanations, show your students the ad format guide deep dive page:

- https://www.facebook.com/business/ads/ad-formats?ref=ads_guide.

From the deep dive, you can select on an ad format to see the best use cases for using that ad format (see example of Photo Ads in Image 13). You will also see a list of best practices for that ad format. It is important to go over these with your students. Show your students a few ad formats that are relevant to your client and class.

Students also need to know the requirements for the different ad formats. These requirements must be adhered to in order to create an ad on the Facebook properties.

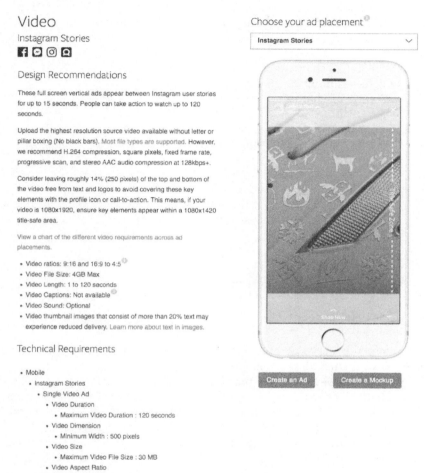

Image 14. Video requirements from https://www.facebook.com/business/ads-guide/video/instagram-story.

From the Facebook ads format page (https://www.facebook.com/business/ads-guide), navigate to the options for visual assets in Facebook platform ads, which are currently: Video, image, carousel, and collection. Each option provides a full list of design and technical requirements as well as other assets needed. The page will also show you which ad placements work with that option. By changing the ad placement option, the requirements will change. At the bottom of the page, there is a list of the advertising objectives each visual option and ad placement combo supports. See the example of a video ad option with an Instagram Stories ad placement in Image 14.

The ad copy text requirements vary depending on the ad format. Share the requirements for the ad formats relevant to your class. For example, a standard image ad in the Facebook feed with an advertising objective of driving traffic to a website requires:

- Headline: 25 characters
- Link description: 30 characters
- Ad Text: 125 characters
- Website URL
- Display Link (optional)
- Call to Action – chosen from a provided list

Lastly, Facebook provides tips for writing ad copy, which will be beneficial to your students:

- https://www.facebook.com/business/news/ad-copy-cheat-sheet.

Why

The why is the same as Learning Objective 1.

How

Before turning your students loose to work on creating their ad(s), familiarize them with social media ads.

If your students completed the Facebook Advertising Case Study assignment from Learning Objective 1, then they have seen some successful Facebook ads. If not, show students example ads in the Facebook Creative Hub Gallery (https://www.facebook.com/ads/creativehub/gallery/). Sort the ads by format using the tags on the page, such as 'image,' 'video,' 'vertical video,' etc. Focus in on the ad formats that are relevant to your client and your class.

Get your students thinking about what social media ads appeal to them. Ask your students to get on Facebook or Instagram. Have them scroll through their feed or stories until they come across a few ads that do or do not appeal to them. Have them take note on what it is about the ad that they do or do not like. Is the ad visually appealing? Did it grab their attention? Does the headline work alongside the visual and the purpose of the ad? What is appealing about the ad text? Does the call to action entice them? Have an open discussion with your students. You can even have your students do screen grabs of the ads and quickly share them with the class by pasting them into a shared Google Doc that you can display on the classroom projector.

In the Create a Social Media Advertisement in the Facebook Creative Hub

Activity, which is discussed in the Do section below, your students will create their first social media ad. If your students are not going to publish these ads and they are completing this assignment for learning purposes only, then I suggest having the students create their ads in the Facebook Creative Hub (see Image 15). This is an easy way to create ad mockups and share them via a link with you or fellow classmates. The ads can even be exported to Facebook Ads Manager for publishing at a later date. This is why I have set up the Create a Social Media Advertisement in the Facebook Creative Hub Activity to be completed in the creative hub.

Your access to graphic design, photography, and video editing software as well as your access to creative from your client will influence what your students can do in terms of designing their ads. The client may be able to provide creative that can be repurposed into ads. You and your students may have the technical skills to use professional software such as Adobe Creative Cloud. If not, I have pasted a list of free resources your students can use to create ad mockups. If your students do not plan to publish these, then focus on the learning aspect of paid social media and do not stress too much over the quality of the multimedia used in the ads.

Free Software for Making Social Media Graphics
- Canva (website and app) - https://www.canva.com/
- Stencil - https://getstencil.com/
- Sprout Social's list of 39 free tools for creating unique images - https://sproutsocial.com/insights/free-image-creation-tools/#design

Free Software for Making and/or Editing Video
- Adobe Spark (web and app) - https://spark.adobe.com/
- Kapwing (web) - https://www.kapwing.com/
- InShot (app): https://apps.apple.com/us/app/inshot-video-editor/id997362197
- iMovie (available on Apple computers)
- Movie Creator (Windows 10)

Free sources for Stock Photos
- Pexels - https://www.pexels.com/
- Pixabay - https://pixabay.com/

Do

Have your students begin building ads by completing the Create a Social Media Advertisement in the Facebook Creative Hub Activity. This activity, available in the chapter appendix, asks the students to create an ad using the parameters the students built and saved in the Create a Campaign and Ad Set in the Facebook Ads Manager Activity during Learning Objective 2. The goal is for the students to create an ad for your client based on the work they have already done to align their ad objective, ad targeting, and other parameters with the client's business goals and the class's social media strategic plan.

To complete this activity, the students will need to log into Facebook Ads Manager with their existing Facebook account. I encourage you to allow students to work on this activity in class so that you can offer guidance.

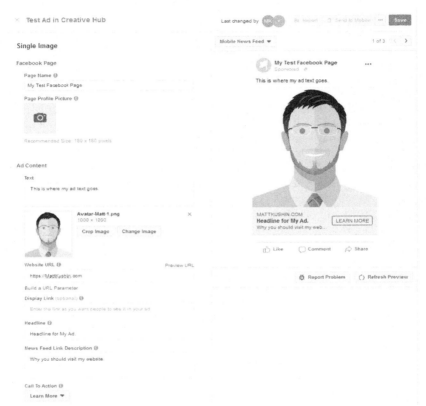

Image 15. A look at how to create an ad mockup in the Facebook Creative Hub. Once completed, these can be exported directly to Facebook Ads Manager or shared via a link.

Reflect

The students reflect on their choices in making their ad through a written reflection in the Create a Social Media Advertisement in the Facebook Creative Hub Activity. But a fun way to get students reflecting on their choices is to choose a few students to share their ads on the classroom projector. This can be done via the shareable link they generated in the activity. Have the students talk through their decisions and ask the rest of the class to play the role of the curious client. Alongside their ads, the students should share the parameters from their Campaign and Ad Set in the Facebook Ads Manager

Activity.

Have your students repeat this activity if you want them to create multiple ads. Recall that if they want to have different ad objectives and/or target audiences, then they will first need to set those up in Facebook Ads Manager. This can be done by having your students repeat the Create a Campaign and Ad Set in the Facebook Ads Manager Activity in Learning Objective 2.

Learning Objective 4: Introducing Campaign Reporting and The Use of Data to Improve Advertising Success

Note: A Few Ways to Approach This Learning Objective

So far, your students have learned how social media advertising works, how to focus on an advertising objective and target an audience, and how to build the creative for an ad. If you have a client with a budget for social media advertising as well as the client's approval, then your class can publish social media ads on the client's behalf and monitor the results. This will help your students learn to use data to better their advertising targeting and success.

Without a client and a budget, it is hard for students to gain hands-on experience. One alternative is to use the Stukent Mimic Social social media marketing simulator (https://www.stukent.com/mimic-social), which contains a section on paid social. This, however, is a product that students pay for. If you do not have a class budget and do not want to use a simulator, then you can still teach your students these concepts and have them learn about campaign results and the use of data to improve advertising through the course "Measure Ad Performance" on Facebook Blueprint. Alternatively, you may want to bring in a guest speaker who can provide a case study in the use of social media advertising.

The below learning objective is set up to provide an introduction to campaign reporting using the Facebook Business suite and some key concepts students should understand on how advertisers can use tools and data to enhance their advertising efforts.

Using the Facebook Pixel

Data from offline and off-Facebook activities can be delivered into Facebook Ads Manager in order to track what actions people take once they click on an ad. This is done through manually uploading data from live events as well as from tools like the Facebook pixel and the Facebook SDK.

Introduce Facebook pixel to your students so they have an understanding of how Facebook tracks behavior outside of Facebook. Facebook pixel is an easy-to-use tool that enables advertisers to track Facebook user's behavior on a website. Behaviors may include things like placing a product in a shopping cart or completing a purchase[29]. Facebook pixel is the tool that your client is most likely to use to track important behaviors on the client's website. Pixel is easy to set up, requiring the addition of a little code to a website, and works with many third-party tools such as Shopify, WordPress, Google Tags Manager and more ("Create and install a Facebook pixel," n.d.). For example, Facebook pixel can be added to WordPress via a simple plugin. It is through the pixel that advertisers track actions from a Facebook ad to the purchase page on a website and thus see the number of conversions the ad produced. This video by Facebook Business offers a quick explanation of how the process works:

- https://youtu.be/vgZ2_qVWLlk.

With pixel, advertisers can also re-target visitors to their website with follow up advertising. Your students will understand what re-targeting is because they have most likely experienced it. Re-targeting is when a person takes an action on a website (e.g., viewing a product) and then sees an ad for that same product later (e.g., on Instagram) ("What is retargeting?," n.d.). Providing students an understanding of how it works can be done through this Facebook Business video:

- https://www.youtube.com/watch?v=sTV5ZysYiRg.

The Facebook pixel is powerful because it lets advertisers track a number of behaviors on a website. Advertisers can use this data to improve their ad targeting. If the client has a marketing sales funnel, then the client can target different audiences with different messages based on where those audience members are in the funnel.

We discussed the marketing sales funnel in Chapter 7 when we discussed social media metrics. But it is worth reviewing. A typical funnel looks something like this:

6. **Reach:** The number of people that may be aware of your message.
7. **Engagement:** The ways in which people interact with your message. This denotes some interest in your message.
8. **Acquisition:** A relationship is built – e.g., a lead is generated, a person subscribes to your email list or blog.
9. **Conversion:** Action is taken – usually, a sale.
10. **Loyalty & Advocacy:** The person buys again, tells someone else about your product, posts a positive review, etc.

By placing pixels on certain webpages that are aligned with stages in the

---

[29] For a full list of standard behaviors that can be tracked with Facebook pixel, see: https://www.facebook.com/business/help/402791146561655?helpref=faq_conte nt.

sales funnel, advertisers can target Facebook users who took those actions on their website with funnel-specific messaging. Here's a simple example.

Funnel Position	We know because person was tracked with:	How do we engage them with a new ad?
Engagement: Person has engaged with your website.	Pixel on all pages of website.	Person is interested in product. Use ad to invite to sign up to learn more.
Acquisition: Person signs up to learn more.	Pixel on email list sign up completion page.	Person is now a lead. Use ad to give limited time discount coupon.
Conversion: Person has bought one product.	Pixel on purchase page.	Use ad to encourage sale of ancillary product.
Loyalty & Advocacy: Person is a repeat customer.	Pixel on purchase page for ancillary product.	Use ad to offer discount to customer for referring friends.

Split Testing and the Test and Learn Tool

Other advanced tools can help advertisers optimize their ad success. A popular tactic in online advertising is split testing, or A/B testing. It's something your students should be aware of. Split testing allows advertisers to see how ads perform when one variable is manipulated and all others are held constant. The variables that can be manipulated are: Ad creative, audience, placement (where the ads are published), and delivery optimization. For example, all of the ad creative could stay consistent but the target audience could be changed from persons in their twenties to persons in their thirties. Or, only the photo in an image ad could be changed, with one photo of a family using a product and one photo of a single person using a product. Facebook Ads Manager has tools built in to manage variables of split testing. You can introduce your students to the concept with this video on the Facebook Business website:

- https://www.facebook.com/business/help/1738164643098669.

Advertisers can also test different bid strategies and compare how they perform. The Test and Learn tool under the Measure and Report column in the Facebook Business Tools suite enables advertisers to run custom tests in order to improve their performance and lower their ad spend.

Ad Reporting

Through the ads manager, Facebook provides ad campaign results for active and completed campaigns. Metrics are determined by the campaign's advertising objective ("Understanding breakdowns, metrics and filtering in ads reporting," n.d.). Common metrics include:

- Reach – Number of people who saw your ad one or more times.
- Impressions – Total views of your ad, which may include the same person seeing it more than once.
- Cost per result – Result is determined by advertising objective. If web traffic was the ad objective, then the cost per result would be calculated based on web traffic generated.
- Amount spent – Estimated spending on an ad during the duration of a campaign.
- Ends – When an ongoing campaign will end.

Cost per result can be weighed against the advertising budget and the desired return on investment. This comes back to the question that should have been posed to the client: What is the desired result worth to the advertiser?

Recall our example of the coffee shop from Learning Objective 1. That shop was willing to spend $.50 to acquire a new customer. Imagine that coffee shop takes online orders and the orders are ready for pick up when the customer arrives. The coffee shop could use a conversion advertising objective and track customers through the online purchase process via a Facebook pixel. An online purchase would thus be a conversion. If the cost per result conversion rate was $.50 or lower, then the coffee shop had a cost per acquisition (CPA) of $.50 or lower. The owner would be happy and the ad campaign would be a success.

Note that we should expect that a cost per result will be lower for low-threshold objectives such as awareness and higher for high-threshold objectives like conversions.

For introductory knowledge into measuring advertising performance, it is important for students to understand ad campaign results metrics, and be able to evaluate campaigns against one another to see which campaigns are driving the desired results at the lowest cost.

Reports can be built to analyze and break down results across variables of interest, such as demographics. See:

- https://www.facebook.com/business/help/487269218011981.

From here, one can move from building and viewing reports to beginning to measure and develop actionable insights through the Ads Reporting tool in the Facebook Business suite. Due to the limited time to teach students about paid social media and the limited time for them to run paid ads for the class client, it is beyond the scope of the class to dive into the Ads Reporting tool[30]. However, the baseline skills learned in this class can be built upon through such advanced tools.

Why

A base understanding of how advertisers use data is an important launching point. It will help students start to think about how data can be used to enhance advertising efforts. It will help them learn to examine and interpret campaign results. Without the ability to extract insights from the data, students cannot tell a client if an ad is having any success nor can they offer suggestions for iterating and improving social media advertising.

How

The How all depends on your class situation. Do you have a client with a budget who wants you to run paid social media ads? Are you going to use a simulator? Do you have a guest speaker with case studies? Is your best available option to walk your students through some of these steps in a demonstration? Do you have access to a webpage where you can embed a Facebook pixel so you can show your students how it works?

Unfortunately, the context of your class varies too widely for me to give you a specific assignment. But here are a few recommendations and activities:

I recommend having your students complete the Facebook Blueprint course "Measure Ad Performance." This is especially important if you are going to have your students publish and manage social media ads for a client.

I also recommend assigning this page in the Facebook Ads Help Center as a reading:

- https://www.facebook.com/business/help/318580098318734.

I've created a knowledge-check activity to help your students actively engage with some of the concepts discussed in this learning objective. The activity is titled Facebook Campaign Reporting and Data Knowledge Check Activity and is available in the chapter appendix.

---

30 If you would like to learn more about generating reports and see the Results and Reporting guide on using ads manager to understand ad performance. I also recommend the "Understanding Campaign Performance with Ads Manager" lesson in the Measure Ad Performance class on Facebook Blueprint.

Do

Set your student teams to work. Each class will differ here depending on how you have chosen to approach this learning objective.

Reflect

However you approach this learning objective, focus on helping your students develop critical thinking and problem solving abilities as they work with any data generated in Facebook Ads Manager. While they are not at an expert level, with a little prodding and challenging, they can begin to develop these abilities and build confidence.

Ask questions like, "What is the most confusing (muddiest) point as you work with this data?"

Show the students data and ask two students to write down their own interpretations of it. Then, get the students to compare these interpretations to see how they might be seeing information differently.

If your student teams run ads, have each group bring its results forward and ask other teams to role-play the client. Assuming the client knows nothing about how to work with Facebook Ads Manager, have the role-playing teams ask for explanation and clarification on findings.

Recommended Readings and More

Facebook Blueprint Courses

Beginner's courses:
- Beyond likes: Create ads that meet your business goals.
  How to create an ad on Facebook
- A beginner's guide to Facebook ad policy
- Find your people on Facebook
- How to set a budget and schedule for your Facebook ads
- The Facebook ad review process

Professional courses:
- Get Started with Advertising
- Target the Right Audience
- Manage Ads
- Measure Ad Performance

Readings

About ad auctions. (n.d.). *Facebook Business.* Retrieved from
https://www.facebook.com/business/help/430291176997542?helpr

ef=faq_content

About ads reporting. (n.d.). *Facebook Business*. Retrieved from
https://www.facebook.com/business/help/487269218011981

About advertising objectives. (n.d.). *Facebook Business*. Retrieved from
https://www.facebook.com/business/help/517257078367892

About split testing. (n.d.). *Facebook Business*. Retrieved from
https://www.facebook.com/business/help/1738164643098669

Ad formats: Find beautiful, powerful ways to tell your business story. (n.d.).
Facebook Business. Retrieved from
https://www.facebook.com/business/ads/ad-formats?ref=ads_guide

Create and install a Facebook Pixel. (n.d.). *Facebook Business*. Retrieved
https://www.facebook.com/business/help/952192354843755

How to use ad relevance diagnostics. (n.d.). *Facebook Blueprint*. Retrieved
from
https://www.facebook.com/business/help/436113280262012?helpr
ef=faq_content.

Facebook ads guide. (n.d.). *Facebook Business*. Retrieved from
https://www.facebook.com/business/ads-guide

Facebook ad objectives: Choose a marketing goal for your ads. (n.d.).
Facebook Business. Retrieved from
https://www.facebook.com/business/ads/ad-objectives#

Glossary of ad terms. (n.d.). *Facebook Business*. Retrieved from
https://www.facebook.com/business/help/447834205249495

The ad copy cheat sheet. (n.d.). *Facebook Business*. Retrieved from
https://www.facebook.com/business/news/ad-copy-cheat-sheet

View results on your Facebook ad in Ads Manager. (n.d.). *Facebook
Business*. Retrieved from
https://www.facebook.com/business/help/318580098318734

Videos

Facebook campaign setup – Campaigns vs. ad sets. vs. ads. (2018,
September 25). Boot Camp Digital. Retrieved from
https://www.youtube.com/watch?time_continue=149&v=LEQtbWOX

dBo

Conversion tracking: A Facebook overview. (2014, August 6). Retrieved from https://youtu.be/vgZ2_qVWLlk

Custom audiences from your website: A Facebook overview. (2014, August 7). Retrieved from https://www.youtube.com/watch?v=sTV5ZysYiRg

Reach relevant people with Facebook ads. (n.d.). *Facebook Business*. Retrieved from https://www.facebook.com/business/learn/lessons/facebook-ad-audience-considerations#

Chapter 8 Appendix

Content Period 3 Assignment

Note to the reader: Provide the Social Media Brand Guidelines to your students (see the Chapter 5 Appendix). These are the same guidelines they should have used in creating their strategic briefs. Recall that the Social Media Grading Rubric can be distributed to students to guide them in creating their content. In fact, I attach it to the bottom of the assignment when I distribute the assignment to my students. You can use it to assist in grading (see the Chapter 5 Appendix).

In the below assignment, modify the time period for which you want the students creating proposed content based on your needs.

The instructions tell the students to organize their content using the content calendar the professor will provide. This is a reference to the Social Media Content Calendar Template referenced in the Chapter 5 Appendix. Make a shareable copy with your students with updated dates to reflect the weeks for which your students will be creating content.

The referenced Social Media Measurement spreadsheet is available in the Chapter 7 Appendix.

Lastly, recall the list of resources provided in Chapter 5 which may help students in designing their social media content (see p. 87).

Overview

Purpose
For Content Period 3, your team will create 1 batch (see definition below) of content which can be spread out <u>over a 5-week period, beginning with finals week</u>.

1. **To Do**
2. Relying on your strategic brief, the monitoring you've done of your social media channel, and any feedback you received regarding your Content Period 2 content:
   - Create content for your social channel for the assigned weeks. Consider any dates, events, or other tie-ins on the calendar for that time frame (e.g., finals week, winter break, etc.).
3. In creating this content, plan to use at least 1 of the influencers your team identified in Content Period 1. Explain your plan in your presentation.
4. Track key metrics each week in the Social Media Measurement spreadsheet I have provided.

5. Create and present a group reflection (see questions below in "group reflections" section).

Content Tasks

You have two tasks:

1. Content Requirements (Quality > quantity)

Organized for the time period assigned in the form of the social media content calendar:

My primary concerns are:

- Each piece of content ties together – it is purposive and fits with the plan you created in your strategic brief assignment.
- You've created audience centric, original content that will stand out.
- It's of a high professional quality (writing, editing, visuals, etc.).

Content Period 3 Batch =

- Blogs: 5 posts spread across the 5 weeks – About ¾ to 1-page double spaced text. Minimum of 2 visuals per post needed.
    - o   For each post you need to provide 2 different promotional tweets. Write these in the content calendar on the day that you want your blog to be published and the day after.
- Instagram, Twitter, Snapchat: 14 posts of ORIGINAL visuals and text

2. Track Metrics

Your team will track key metrics for your social channel.
Turn in the final version when submitting your assignment materials.
How? Download a copy in .XLS format and add to zip file.

Grading Criteria

- Appropriateness of work to the situation, audience, and client
- Professional quality of content
- Extent to which content is consistent with project goals
- Extent to which content is consistent with team's strategy as put forth in their strategic brief
- Considers/adapts to feedback given by professor

Presentation Tasks

Your group will present your content in a professional setting to the class.
Time: About 12 minutes of presentation time.

Be sure to address:

1. Content:
    a. How your content fits with your content categories (i.e., your 'content buckets').
    b. How your content takes into consideration the monitoring

you've done of your social media channel, and any feedback you received via your content periods 1 and 2 from the professor and your peers.

2. **Metrics:**
    a. For your metrics: Benchmarks, KPIs, week when KPIs were reached, and what the metric was that week (if reached), final metrics.
    b. In terms of optimization: What variables (e.g., hashtags, photo versus video, etc.) are associated with posts that are getting higher engagement?
    c. For social listening: How has the conversation around the client changed over the weeks? What has been consistent?
    d. Analyzing and interpreting all the data you tracked, answer: What actions could your client take with this knowledge?
3. **Group Reflection** – An opportunity to share what you learned with the class. Consider:
    a. What were the highlights – the things you were most proud of?
    b. What would you have done better?
    c. What were the biggest challenges you faced? How did you overcome them? Or were you not able to?
    d. What would you have done differently, if you had a chance to start over again?
    e. What did you learn from the project in regard to social media and its use by organizations?
        i. Some areas that may be good to discuss: Audiences, content planning, engagement, metrics, etc.
    f. What recommendations do you have for the client to help them run their social media successfully in the future?

Q&A / Evaluation
Afterwards, your classmates (who are roleplaying as the client) will evaluate your presentation and will be encouraged to ask you questions.

Expectations
Do not treat this as a presentation for a class. Treat it as a presentation at your job.
- Business casual (jeans or khakis, "polo" shirt or nicer).
- Polished, practiced, professional presentation style.
- Presentations more than two minutes outside of the time window will receive a grade deduction.

Facebook Advertising Case Study Presentation Assignment (Without Facebook IQ)

Note to the reader: This is a shorter version of the Facebook Advertising Case Study Presentation assignment. A longer version of this assignment is available in Chapter 9.

To prepare my students to complete the below assignment, I require that they complete a few lessons on Facebook Blueprint (https://www.facebookblueprint.com/student/catalog). They are listed in the assignment.

To do

Your team will complete a case study activity exploring Facebook advertising. Via a presentation to the class, you will analyze the cases and offer insights and interpretations.

Preparation

You should complete the below Facebook Blueprint courses to prepare for this assignment:
1. Get Started with Advertising
2. Target the Right Audience
3. Measure Ad Performance
4. Choose 1 course from the list of lessons from with ANY 1 of these categories: "Build awareness," "Drive consideration," "Generate leads," "Promote my app," "Manage ads," "Increase online sales."

Instructions

There are several parts to this assignment. Work in your team in a manner that is fair:

- Part 1: Identify an example of a successful Facebook ad campaign by browsing https://www.facebook.com/ads/creativehub/gallery/.
    - If you're having a hard time accessing it, make sure you are logged out of the Facebook Business Tools.
    - Show the class the ad and educate the class about the campaign. To do so, you'll need to research it. If you can't find much about it, then pick another campaign.
        - Example: For the BMW 4in4 created by FCB Inferno ad agency, I googled "BMW 4in4" and a few other things and found lots of great insights.
- Part 2: Using the ad campaign from Part 1, conduct Facebook Audience Insights research (at https://www.facebook.com/ads/creativehub, log in with Facebook and then select 'audience insights' from the menu) into the audience that already likes that company on Facebook (watch the tutorial video listed in the resources below).
    - Provide a breakdown of key takeaways of their audience across demographics, page likes, location and activity.
- Part 3: Given what you know from Part 2 above, if you were creating a

new Facebook Ad targeting this audience (explain briefly for each below):

- o What age range would you target?
- o What gender(s) would you target?
- o Which is the primary country and city you would target?
- o What is a bit of information from the page likes, interests, etc. that might help you in targeting or planning your ad?

In addressing the sections above, consider these questions:
- What would you do with this information?
- What are the main points we should be aware of?
- What ideas can we get from this data?
- How could you use this information to begin planning for a new Facebook or Instagram ad campaign for this brand?

Resources
- Facebook Audience Insights Tutorial Video (will show you how to use the tool): https://youtu.be/KDMTkR_8ozM

Expectations
Visuals – e.g., Show us the content you've created.
Use slides (You will turn your slides in). Slides must contain:
- All names of group members
- All visuals, including screen grabs from your Facebook Audience Insights research
- Links to the Facebook ad from Part 1
- List of all sources used in your research at the end of your slides – you can simply provide URLs.

Presentation length: About 5-7 minutes
Presentation should include all members.

Grading Criteria
Your presentation style may be conversational. However, be sure to know what you are talking about and be prepared. Deductions for signs that teammates are not on the same page or uncertain of their role in presentation, who talks when, etc.

Create a Campaign and Ads Set in the Facebook Ads Manager Activity

Overview

You will learn to use the Facebook Ads Manager tool to plan a paid social media advertisement.

Getting Started
1. Go to Facebook Ads Manager and login with your Facebook account: https://www.facebook.com/business/tools/ads-manager
2. Once logged in, click the menu button and select "Ads Manager."
3. Choose the campaign tab and click the green create button (see image below).

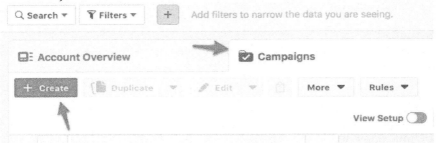

Tasks
Considering our class client's goals and objectives, your team's strategic brief, and any instruction I provided you, complete the following:

Step 1: Advertising Objective
- Before creating your ad, you need to set up your campaign. To do so:
  - Choose your advertising objective from the list of options provided.
  - Give your campaign a name.
    - You can leave any other options set to off.
  - Click continue.

Step 2: Build Your Targeted Audience
You are now in the ad sets portion of Facebook Ads Manager, which means you will determine the audience and other important information for your ad.
- Use the audience options to define your target audience.
- Click "save this audience" and give your audience a name so you can use this audience later if you create more ads.

Step 3: Select Ad Placements
- Select the ad placements, that is, where you want your ads to be

displayed across the Facebook properties, which include Facebook, Instagram, Facebook Messenger, and more. You can choose:
- o   Automated placements – which will automatically place your ad across the Facebook properties, or:
- o   Edit Placements – which allows you to manually select which placements you want to use.

Step 4: Set Your Budget
- If you see a dropdown menu for 'optimization for ad delivery,' you can leave it as is. Facebook selects the most preferred optimized pricing model based on your ad objective.
- For now, if you see a cost control option, leave it empty. We did not cover this in class.
- Determine a daily or lifetime budget and select a start and end date.

Click "close" and select "safe as draft." If you don't, your work will not be saved.

Reflection and Submitting Your Work
When you're done, create a document and answer the below questions to turn in:
1. What advertising objective did you choose and why?
2. List the audience variables you chose. Write a brief rationale for your audience targeting. Be sure to note:
   a.   Location
   b.   Age
   c.   Gender
   d.   Languages
   e.   All detailed targeting: include categories and/or subcategories.
3. Provide a screen grab of the Audience Size and Estimated Daily Results (see image to the right).
4. What ad placements did you choose and why?
5. What budget did you set? Explain your reasoning.

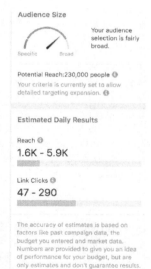

Audience Size

Your audience selection is fairly broad.

Specific   Broad

Potential Reach:230,000 people

Your criteria is currently set to allow detailed targeting expansion.

Estimated Daily Results

Reach

1.6K - 5.9K

Link Clicks

47 - 290

The accuracy of estimates is based on factors like past campaign data, the budget you entered and market data. Numbers are provided to give you an idea of performance for your budget, but are only estimates and don't guarantee results.

Create a Social Media Advertisement in the Facebook Creative Hub Activity

Overview

You will learn to use the Facebook Creative Hub tool to create a paid social media advertisement. The advertisement will be based on the campaign and ad set parameters you set up in the Create a Campaign and Ads Set in the Facebook Ads Manager Activity. The goal is to create an ad for your client.

Resources
Use Facebook's ad copy cheat sheet when writing your ad copy: https://www.facebook.com/business/news/ad-copy-cheat-sheet.

Getting Started

1. Go to Facebook Ads Manager and log in with your Facebook account: https://www.facebook.com/business/tools/ads-manager
2. Once logged in, click the menu button and select "Creative Hub."
3. Click, "Create Mockup."
4. Choose the ad format that you want to create from the provided list (see image to the right).
5. Use our client as the Facebook page and upload their page profile picture.
6. Follow the prompts to build your ad. You can change how the ad displays across mobile and desktop through a dropdown menu on the page.
7. When you're done, click save.

Reflection and Submitting Your Work
To turn your assignment in, click the menu button next to the "Save Changes" button. A dropdown menu will appear (see image below). Click "Copy Link." Turn that link in to me along with a brief, written rationale for your ad. Be sure explain your rationale for the visuals you used, the headline you wrote, the ad text, and the call to action.

Facebook Campaign Reporting and Data Knowledge Check Activity

Note to the reader: A model answer for part 2 of this activity is:

Test 1: Variable – audience.
They could test different ages to see if their ad produces higher conversions with different age ranges. For example, they could test ages: 14-17, 25-30, 31-35.

Test 2: Variable – placement.
They could run the same ad targeting the same audience on Instagram as well as other Facebook properties, such as Facebook or the Facebook Advertising Network, to see how the ad performs.

A model answer for part 3 is below:
The answer is Ad 1. Ad 1 costs less than $3 per result. Each result is a conversion (i.e., sale of a shoe). While Ad 2 cost less money, and cost less per impression, it did not achieve the result.

Note that some students may have been distracted by the instructions to "get the most bang for their buck." They may have even taken steps to determine the cost per impressions (CPM), thinking that the most eyeballs per dollar was the best way to think about this problem. But the purpose (that is, how 'bang for their buck' was defined) was to meet the <$3 cost per acquisition (i.e., conversion) and not to optimize for impressions. Still, here's the math on CMP in case any of your students present it:
We know Ad 2 cost less per 1,000 impressions. Here's how: CPM =)[cost of advertising] / [impressions]) x 1,000.

Ad 1 CPM = (2,000 / 32,000) x 1,000 = $62.50
Ad 2 CPM = (275 / 52,50) x 1,000 = $52.38

So, for Ad 2, there were a lot of impressions but fewer people were converting.

Scenario
Imagine you are running a paid social media campaign for a company that sells a stylish but casual waterproof shoe. It's called Wow Shoes.
Wow Shoes wants you to develop advertisements based on custom audiences developed through data available through the Facebook pixel that is installed on their website. A custom audience is an audience that is built using data from Facebook pixels, such as "people who have added our shoes to their shopping cart (but did not purchase)."

Part 1: Facebook Pixel and the Marketing Sales Funnel

There are 2 audiences Wow Shoes wants to target and a reason for each:
1. Custom Audience 1: People who have been to our website previously.
   a. Reason: They know about our products and thus may be interested in them.
2. Custom Audience 2: People who have bought a pair of our winter shoes before.
   a. Reason: The new spring line of shoes is out.

Tasks to Complete
Use the resources and examples below to help you:
1. Determine where each audience is in the marketing sales funnel.
2. Answer: How do we engage each audience via a new ad?

Resources and Examples
The marketing sales funnel:
11. **Reach:** The number of people that may be aware of your message.
12. **Engagement:** The ways in which people interact with your message. This denotes some interest in your message.
13. **Acquisition:** A relationship is built – e.g., a lead is generated, a person subscribes to your email list or blog.
14. **Conversion:** Action is taken – usually, a sale.
15. **Loyalty & Advocacy:** The person buys again, tells someone else about your product, etc.

Examples:
Here's an example of 2 audiences across 2 positions in the marketing sales funnel and how we could engage them with a new ad.

Funnel Position	We know because person was tracked with:	How do we engage them with a new ad?
Acquisition: Person signs up to learn more.	Pixel on email list sign up completion page.	Person is now a lead. Use ad to give limited time discount coupon.
Loyalty & Advocacy: Person is a repeat customer.	Pixel on purchase page for add on item to a product we create and sell.	Use ad to offer discount to customer for referring friends.

Part 2: Split Testing
Wow Shoes has always targeted persons aged 18 to 24 with their social media advertising. They also only run their ads on Instagram, assuming that their target audience uses Instagram the most.
How could they use split testing to test their assumptions? What variables could they split test?

Part 3: Ad Results

You ran a social media ad campaign for Wow Shoes.

The campaign goal was to convert the target audience to buy a $100 pair of shoes. The company asked you to run 2 ads. The results are below:

Each ad is optimized for a result of conversions.

Ad 1 Results:
- Reach – 20,000
- Impressions – 32,000
- Cost per result – $2.56
- Amount spent – $2,000

Ad 2 Results:
- Reach – 3,800
- Impressions – 5,250
- Cost per result – $3.25
- Amount spent – $275

They want to run more ads and get the most bang for their buck. For these new ads, Wow Shoes has told you that they need to spend $3 or less on advertising for each shoe they sell.

Which ad would you recommend they run again, if any (explain your answer?)

Matthew J. Kushin, Ph.D.

CHAPTER 9: BONUS ASSIGNMENTS

Because, who doesn't love extras?

Unfortunately, there is only so much time in a semester; only so much that can be done in one class. I wrote this book to cover how you can organize an entire semester around running your class as a quasi-agency. However, there are several things that I cover in my social media class that did not fit squarely into the model above. For example, there are side tangents, like lectures on theories of social networking and more in depth discussions of diffusion of innovations.

I'm not going to cover all of them here, because this is your class and these empty spaces are your spaces. I want you to fill those spaces with the content that is most relevant to your students, at your university, under your expertise. Further, each of us is different and we teach at different speeds. So you may find that, upon covering the material in the preceding chapters, there are no empty spaces to fill.

But, if there are empty spaces, then the brief chapter below will provide you with a few additional assignments and activities that you may enjoy and which may benefit your students. These are not organized in the What, Why, How, Do, Reflect Framework that served as the centerpiece of this book. In fact, this chapter isn't as much of a chapter as it is an appendix to this book. The assignments are simply listed.

Case Study Paper and Presentation

To do

Find an organization's social media campaign to analyze.

Look for articles, posts, or other write ups that provide sufficient detail to complete the assignment.

Some examples (You can't use these. They are outdated.):
- Tide
- Audi Super Bowl 2014

Some great sources (there are many more!):
- Mashable, SpinSucks, Adweek, Fast Company, SocialMediaExplorer, PR Week case studies (creating a free account should give you access to the case studies on the left), PR Newser, Council on Public Relations Firms.

Format
- ~5 pages, double spaced (grade reduction for over/under 1/2 page)
- Organize using headers
- Sources: Links to all sources used in a reference at bottom of paper.

Paper Requirements
- 5 sources needed – include articles about the case your paper is on. You must include reference to at least 1 of the class books. You can also use assigned readings, additional academic research or industry texts.
- In text citations for your sources are needed to bolster your claims.

Your Paper Should be organized as Follows
1. Overview of the campaign:
    a. Include: The situation (problem, opportunity – such as the Super Bowl, or a crisis), objectives (the purpose of the campaign – what it was trying to achieve), when it occurred, social channels used, and any other key overview information.
2. Understanding Audience:
    a. Who is the target audience for this campaign? (if it is not overtly stated, who can you surmise it is?)
    b. Monitoring: How did the organization learn about and/or track their audience? (If this isn't stated, how could they have based on what you've learned?)
3. Strategy and Content:
    a. What was their strategy for this campaign (e.g., What did they decide to do? How did they go about planning and executing it?)
    b. What content did they create to execute their strategy?
        i. What platforms did they use to push their content?

          ii.   If they mention content optimization, explain.

4.   Measurement:
- a.   What metrics were they interested in / or did / do they measure? (If none stated, based on what you learned in class – refer to your class notes - , what would be logical metrics for them to be measuring?)
- b.   If no metrics are present, try some of the analytics tools you have learned in this class to search this campaign.

5.   Ethics and Social Issues: Choose 1 of the following – either ethics or social issues (don't write about both):
- a.   Ethics: Discuss ethical considerations related to this campaign.
  - i.   What ethical issues do you think the organization needs to consider in planning their campaign? Were they effective in dealing with them? What ethical concerns or problems do you have that could arise from their campaign?
- b.   Social and Cultural Issues
  - i.   Considering the Frontline "Generation Like" and assigned readings, including: http://bit.ly/FSM_socialmediaissues
    - 1.   What social or cultural issues discussed in the Frontline video or the readings relate to this campaign? What action is this company taking that should the consumer be wary of? What are possible effects of these actions, and why should we be concerned?

5)   Analysis and Recommendation:
- a.   Analysis: What are the pros and cons of this campaign? (What worked, what didn't?)
- b.   How would you revise or improve this campaign? What should they consider going forward?
  - i.   Cite sources from course readings or your own research to support your claims.

6)   Sources: List of all sources used, including links to the article(s) analyzed in this piece.

Facebook Advertising Case Study Presentation (With Facebook IQ)

Note to the reader: This is a longer version of the Facebook Advertising Case Study Presentation assignment which is available in the Chapter 8 Appendix. It requires students to conduct research on the Facebook IQ website.

To prepare my students to complete the below assignment, I require that they complete a few lessons on Facebook Blueprint (https://www.facebookblueprint.com/student/catalog). They are listed in the assignment.

To do
Your team will complete a case study activity exploring Facebook advertising. Via a presentation to the class, you will analyze the case and offer insights and interpretations.

Preparation
You should complete the below Facebook Blueprint courses to prepare for this assignment:
1. Get Started with Advertising
2. Target the Right Audience
3. Measure Ad Performance
4. Choose 1 course from the list of lessons from with ANY 1 of these categories: "build awareness," "Drive consideration," "generate leads," "promote my app," "Manage ads," "Increase online sales."

Instructions
There are 5 parts to this assignment. Work in your team in a manner that is fair:

- Part 1: Go to: https://www.facebook.com/iq. Click "Insights" at the top of the page. Pick an article from the "People Insights"-> topic: "Audience" section in the Facebook IQ data and educate the class about it.
- Part 2: Go to: https://www.facebook.com/iq. Click "Insights" at the top of the page. Pick an article from the topics under either "Advertising Insights" or "Industry Insights" that is RELATED to the audience insights you chose in some way (from Part 1). Educate the class about it.
- Part 3: Identify an example of a successful Facebook ad campaign by browsing https://www.facebook.com/ads/creativehub/gallery/.
  - Note: It would be ideal to find something related to parts 1 and 2 of your project. But, it may not be possible.
  - If you're having a hard time accessing it, make sure you are logged out of Facebook Creative Hub.
  - o Show the class the ad and educate the class about the campaign. To do so, you'll need to research it. If you can't find much about it, then pick another campaign.

- Example: For the BMW 4in4 created by FCB Inferno ad agency, I googled "BMW 4in4" and a few other things and found lots of great insights.
- Part 4: Using the ad campaign from Part 3, conduct Facebook Audience Insights research (at https://www.facebook.com/ads/creativehub, log in with Facebook and then select 'audience insights' from the menu) into the audience that already likes that company on Facebook (watch the tutorial video listed in the resources below).
  - Provide a breakdown of key takeaways of their audience across demographics, page likes, location and activity.
- Part 5: Given what you know from Part 4 above, if you were creating a new Facebook Ad targeting this audience (explain briefly for each below):
  - What age range would you target?
  - What gender(s) would you target?
  - Which is the primary country and city you would target?
  - What is a bit of information from the page likes, interests, etc. that might help you in targeting or planning your ad?

In addressing the sections above, consider these questions:
- What would you do with this information?
- What are the main points we should be aware of?
- What ideas can we get from this data?
- How could you use this information to begin planning for a new Facebook or Instagram ad campaign for this brand?

Resources
- Facebook Audience Insights Tutorial Video (will show you how to use the tool): https://youtu.be/KDMTkR_8ozM

Expectations
Visuals – e.g., Show us the content you've created.
Use slides (You will turn your slides in). Slides must contain:
- All names of group members
- All visuals, including screen grabs from your Facebook Audience Insights research
- Links to the Facebook ad from Part 1
- List of all sources used in your research at the end of your slides – you can simply provide URLs.
Presentation length: About 5-7 minutes
Presentation should include all members.

Grading Criteria
Your presentation style may be conversational. However, be sure to know what you are talking about and be prepared. Deductions for signs that

teammates are not on the same page or uncertain of their role in presentation, who talks when, etc.

Industry and Software Certifications and Educational Programs

These certifications can be integrated into your class or can be assigned as standalone assignments for your students to complete outside of class. They can also be made available for extra credit. Popular certifications include:

Name	Link to Certification
Bing Ads Certification	https://about.ads.microsoft.com/en-us/resources/training/get-accredited
Google Analytics	https://support.google.com/google-ads/answer/6089828?hl=en
Google Adwords Certification	https://support.google.com/google-ads/answer/9029201?hl=en
Hootsuite	https://support.google.com/google-ads/answer/9029201?hl=en
HubSpot Academy	https://academy.hubspot.com/certification-overview
Facebook Blueprint	https://www.facebook.com/business/learn (note: While the education materials are free, the certification cost money).
SEMRush Academy	https://www.semrush.com/academy/courses/33/info
Twitter Flight School	https://flightschool.twitter.com/

Personal Branding Assignment

Note to the reader: The inspiration for this assignment came from A Roadmap for Teaching Social Media: All the assignments, rubrics, and feedback guides you'll need to present a strategic social media course! *by Karen Freberg. Several of the tips below are adapted from that book. They have been printed with permission by Karen Freberg.*

Overview

The purpose of this assignment is to help you get started with personal branding and networking online by applying concepts you learned in class.

First, read this article – it is worth your time:

- https://www.linkedin.com/pulse/move-over-resume-networking-key-success-pr-social-media-karen-freberg

Instructions

Getting Started (this is for your own use. You don't have to turn it into me. However, not working through this checklist will vastly diminish your success).

Dr. Freberg's Personal Branding Checklist and Tips quoted from *A Roadmap for Teaching Social Media.*

Work through the below.

Who are you as a person?
- What's your story? What makes you "you"?
- Your background? Hobbies, interests?
- Key experiences, perspectives, expertise that you have to share?
- What are your strengths/weaknesses – and what steps can you take to improve?

Professional passion?
- How are you different from other students? Other people who have similar goals or skills as you?
- What are 3-5 topics you can focus on to establish yourself as a thought leader in the community, a profession, or on social media?

Overarching theme or message you want brands, practitioners and professional in the industry to know?
- What are the main areas of expertise you want professionals to know you have?

- Construct a list of professionals, brands, blogs, Twitter handles, etc. you want to engage with online
    - List key influencers in the industry you want to work in – sites like http://buzzsumo.com/ can help.
    - List agencies, brands, etc. you want to work for.
    - Are there online Twitter chats, etc. or discussion boards you can join?

What's Due? (Everything italicized below):

Part 1: Find an internship or job
Some sites to check (probably your best place to start!):
    - Jobs (but look for an entry level position, not manager or director):
        - https://jobs.prsa.org/jobs/
        - http://meojobsonline.com/blog/project/jobsoftheday/
        - SocialMediaJobs.com
        - PRSA.org/jobcenter
        - prnewsonline.com/resources/pr_jobs.html
        - HooJobs.com

Describe: Drop a link to the position. What is the position? You can tell me in a sentence or 2.
1. *How does this position align with your existing skill set? Explain.*
2. *What skills do you need to complete this job? What can you do to work on getting those skills?*

Part 2: Map out your personal brand using some of the key terms you learned this semester. In a document, determine the below:

1. *Voice: What is your tone?*
    a. *To consider: friendly, serious, humorous, erudite? How will you show it to the community?*
2. *3-5 Influencers – Using bullet points, list their username, social platform, and a brief rationale.*
    a. *To consider: Who are the people you want to connect with online who can mentor, educate and be part of your community? Do some searching.*
3. *Goal: What is your primary goal?*
    a. *Example: Become a thought leader in the drone racing community; get into grad school; work at a specific company; become a world famous musician; create a YouTube cooking channel; become a social media influencer*

in fashion, etc.

4. *2-3 Key Messages and Message Support*
   a. *These are key messages about YOU. That is, what are the key messages about Brand You that you want to convey to others? And, what evidence do you have to support these messages?*
      i. *They are not about the company itself. They are about YOU.*
5. *2 Objectives – for you to achieve your goal.*
   a. *Remember to write S.M.A.R.T. objectives. Your objectives are measurable outcomes you need to achieve by a point in time that help you accomplish your goal.*
      i. *Ex: Earn an internship with Vanity Fair for summer 2021; Build a following of 3,000 people on my YouTube page by December 2022.*
6. *Strategies and Tactics – however many you find you need – Recall, a strategy is your plan for achieving your objective. And tactics are the steps or tasks needed to complete your strategy.*
   a. *Ex: Strategy: Develop a "College cooking" YouTube series featuring popular musicians on college radio stations*
      i. *Ex: Tactic: Identify musicians; contact with request to join my show; create episode schedule; shoot episodes; etc. etc.*

Part 3: Build Your Profiles

Step 1: Look over what you're currently posting on social media. If your social media use isn't professional, now is your opportunity to change that.

I use the "grandma test." That means, I don't publish anything I wouldn't want my sweet, loving grandmother to see.

Step 2: While I encourage you to be professionally active on many social networks, particularly those relevant to your goals, you are required to either 1) create a professional, public LinkedIn account for this class or 2) an about.me page. It must contain:

1. Name your page accordingly (ex: about.me/yourname or linkedin.com/in/yourname). Think about your professional identity online. If you have a somewhat common name, it can be hard to find you online. Perhaps you want to use a middle name or an abbreviated version of your name to distinguish yourself.
2. A professional headshot – Don't have one? Find a friend (maybe someone from this class) with some photo skills and ask them to take a photo of you. Do not use a casual photo or a photo with people other than you in it. It must be professional in nature.
   a. Tip: Be consistent with your visuals by using the same

headshot across your online assets.
3. Tagline (LinkedIn): You can put your title or a tagline instead of your title. Ex: Dr. Carolyn Mae Kim uses "Developer. Strategist. Professor" on her LinkedIn page.
4. In your profile section: Provide your elevator statement or a summary of your skills and accomplishments.
5. Enumerate membership in clubs, organization, volunteering, jobs, or other experience relevant to your goals.

Paste the link to your LinkedIn or about.me page into the bottom of the document you turn into me. Any non-public pages (meaning, pages I can't access without a password) will receive a -15%.

Note: If you don't want this info to stay public, just make it public for the duration of this assignment and make it private or delete it after this assignment has been graded.

Examples:
Dr. Freberg's LinkedIn profile: https://www.linkedin.com/in/karenfreberg
Dr. Kushin's LinkedIn profile: https://www.linkedin.com/in/mattkushin
Dr. Zhang's website: https://www.aiaddysonzhang.com/

Part 4: Execute - Begin engaging your audience and building your brand

To Do
Get connected:
*   Identify the social media platforms most relevant to your field. E.g., Twitter is very popular among reporters; Instagram among photographers; blogs among writers; etc.
    o   Follow relevant brands, industry outlets, influencers, etc.
    o   Follow others who are mentioned among those you respect and admire in your community
    o   Non-profits, brands, professionals, influencers, etc.
    o   Find Twitter chats you can join
        ▪   Directory: http://twubs.com/twitter-chats

Pay it Forward:
*   Think about who you want to reach and share timely resources that they can benefit from.
    o   Practice curation:
        ▪   Share work of those you admire. The best way to get traffic is to share the content of those you want to notice you.
        ▪   Give credit to originators of content.
        ▪   Provide comments / feedback on posts by those

with whom you want to network.
- o Share:
  - Blog posts
  - Resources
  - Tutorials
  - Lists and best practices
  - Podcasts, videos, slideshares, etc.
- o Congratulate others on accomplishments and give shout outs to others.
- Engage the Community
  - o Connect with influences. Don't be afraid to start the conversation.
  - o Read and respond/share content from those you've identified.
  - o Seek out mentors. Connect. Don't be afraid to ask for help.
- Monitor Your Engagement
  - o Monitor what of your content gets shared, and make more of it/share more of it.
  - o Respond to comments.
  - o Show personality

Thinking through the "to do" bullet points above, write me a brief paragraph or 2 describing what and how you have taken steps/are beginning to take steps towards executing. Paste in screen grabs as evidence when possible/appropriate to support your points.

As Boyz II Men once sang, we've come "to the end of the road" (Yes, I just did that. :P After all, I'm a child of the 90s).

You made it. Give yourself a high five!

Thank you for reading this book. I hope it helps you #TeachConfident when you build your hands-on, engaged social media class. You got this!

This book was a labor of love and I hope you enjoyed it. If you did, please share a photo of your copy on social media and say hello by tagging me: @mjkushin on Twitter, @mattkushin on Linkedin, and @mjkushin on Instagram.

I hope you will review it on Amazon and/or Goodreads.

I truly appreciate you.

Matthew J. Kushin, Ph.D.

References

About ad auctions. (n.d.). *Facebook Business*. Retrieved from
https://www.facebook.com/business/help/430291176997542?helpr
ef=faq_content

About advertising objectives. (n.d.). Facebook Business. Retrieved from
https://www.facebook.com/business/help/517257078367892

Ad auction and delivery overview. (2018, September 25). *Facebook
Blueprint*. Retrieved from
https://www.facebookblueprint.com/student/activity/176651-ad-
auction-and-delivery-overview

Audience network: Create an ad on Facebook. Show it across the Web. (n.d.).
Facebook Business. Retrieved from
https://www.facebook.com/business/marketing/audience-network

Addyson-Zhang, A. (2019, April 18). Using livestreaming to grow your
brand, community, & influence. Shonali Burke. Retrieved from
https://shonaliburke.com/using-livestreaming-to-grow-your-brand-
community-influence/

Bain, P. (2019, February 5). 10 need to know Facebook marketing stats for
2019. *Social Media Today*. Retrieved from
https://www.socialmediatoday.com/news/10-need-to-know-
facebook-marketing-stats-for-2019/547488/

Berger, J. & Milkman, K.L. (2012). What makes online content viral? *Journal
of Marketing Research*, 49, 192-205.

Berger, Jonah and Eric Schwartz (2011), What Drives Immediate and
Ongoing Word of Mouth? *Journal of Marketing Research*, October, 869-
880.

Berger, J. (2016). *Contagious: Why Things Catch On*. New York, New York:
Simon & Shuster.

Bobbitt, R., Sullivan, R. (2014). *Developing the public relations Campaign: A
team-based approach* (3rd ed.). Boston, MA: Pearson

Boland, B. (2014, June 5). Organic reach on Facebook: Your questions
Answered. *Facebook Business*. Retrieved from
https://www.facebook.com/business/news/Organic-Reach-on-

Facebook

Brito, M. (2013). Your brand, *The Next Media Company: How a Social Business Strategy Enables Better Content, Smarter Marketing, and Deeper Customer Relationships*. Indianapolis, Indiana: Que.

Broom, G.M., & Sha, B.L. (2013). *Cutlip & Center's Effective Public Relations* (11th ed.). Boston, MA: Pearson.

Butler, J. (2017, June 8). Facebook organic reach is deicing. Here's 6 ways to fight it. *Adgo*. Retrieved from https://www.adgo.io/blog/2017/6/8/facebook-organic-reach-is-declining-heres-6-ways-to-fight-it

Carter, R. (2017, December 19). Social media contests in 2018: Do they still work? *Sprout Social*. Retrieved from https://sproutsocial.com/insights/social-media-contests/.

Clampitt, P.G. (2018). *Social Media Strategy: Tools for Professionals and Organizations*. Thousand Oaks, CA: Sage.

Create and install a Facebook Pixel. (n.d.). *Facebook Business*. Retrieved https://www.facebook.com/business/help/952192354843755

Dalisay, F., Kushin, M.J. & Yamamoto, M. (2017). Sentiment Analysis. In L.A. Schintler & C.L. McNeely (Eds.), *Encyclopedia of Big Data*. Springer International Publishing.

Damon, W. (1984). Peer education: The untapped potential. J*ournal of Applied Developmental Psychology, 5*(4), 331-343.

Dichter, E. (1966). How word-of-mouth advertising works. *Harvard Business Review*, 44, 147-166

Erskine, R. (2018, August 13). Facebook engagement sharply drops 50% over last 18 months. *Forbes*. Retrieved from https://www.forbes.com/sites/ryanerskine/2018/08/13/study-facebook-engagement-sharply-drops-50-over-last-18-months/#6fe47fd094e8

Facebook ads: Reach out to future customers and fans. (n.d.). *Facebook Business*. Retrieved from https://www.facebook.com/business/ads

Facebook ad objectives: Choose a marketing goal for your ads. (n.d.). *Facebook Business*. Retrieved from https://www.facebook.com/business/ads/ad-objectives#

Field, H. (2019, April 4). 'Influencer fraud' costs companies millions of dollars. An AI-powered tool can now show who paid to boost their engagement. *Entrepreneur*. Retrieved from https://www.entrepreneur.com/article/331719

Gesenhues, A. (2019a, March 12). Facebook to replace relevance score with 3 new metrics in April: Beginning April 30, Facebook is ending relevance scores and shuttering six other metrics. *Marketing Land*. Retrieved from https://marketingland.com/facebook-to-replace-relevance-score-with-3-new-metrics-in-april-258355

Gesenhues, A. (2019b, May 6). Instagram influencers posting 150% more sponsored content than a year ago. *Marketing Land*. Retrieved from https://marketingland.com/instagram-influencers-posting-150-more-sponsored-content-than-a-year-ago-260445/

Goldschein, E. (2019, March 24). The non-writers' guide to writing better social media copy. *Social Media Today*. Retrieved from https://www.socialmediatoday.com/news/the-non-writers-guide-to-writing-better-social-media-copy/551143/

Goncalves, J., Kostakos, V., & Venkatanathan, J. (2013, August). Narrowcasting in social media: Effects and perceptions. Paper presented at the IEEE/ACM International Conference on Advances in Social Networks Analysis and Mining. Niagara, Canada. Retrieved from: https://www.researchgate.net/publication/259638282_Narrowcasting_in_Social_Media_Effects_and_Perceptions

Hasell, A., & Weeks, B.E. (2016). Partisan provocation: The role of partisan news use and emotional responses in political information sharing in social media. *Human Communication Research, 42*, 641-661.

Heath, C. & Heath, D. (2007). *Made to Stick: Why Some Ideas Survive and Others Die*. New York, NY: Random House.

Hickman, A. (2018, September 26). 'Influencers aren't effective for product marketing' – Edelman's head of influencer. *PR Week*. Retrieved from https://www.prweek.com/article/1494047/influencers-arent-effective-product-marketing-edelmans-head-influencer

Jackson, D. (n.d.). Know your limit: The ideal length of every social media post. *Sprout Social*. Retrieved from https://sproutsocial.com/insights/social-media-character-counter/

Kim, C. M. (2016). *Social Media Campaigns: Strategies for Public Relations and Marketing.* New York, NY: Routledge.

Kaushik, A. (2011, Oct. 10). Best social media metrics: Conversation, amplification, applause, economic value. *Occam's Razor.* Retrieved from https://www.kaushik.net/avinash/best-social-media-metrics-conversation-amplification-applause-economic-value/

Koughan, F. & Rushkoff, D. (Writers), Mangini, T. (Director). (February 18, 2014). Generation Like [Television series episode]. In D. Fanning (Producer). *Frontline.* Boston, Massachusetts: WGBH/Boston.

Liu, J., Li, C., Ji, Y. G., North, M., & Yang, F. (2017). Like it or not: The Fortune 500's Facebook strategies to generate users' electronic word-of-mouth. *Computers in Human Behavior, 73,* 605–613.

Lowery, S.A., & DeFluer, M.L. (1995). *Milestones in mass communication research: Media effects* (3rd ed.). White Plains, N.Y.: Longman Publishers.

Lunden, I. (2019, February 11). LinkedIn debuts LinkedIn Live, a new live video broadcast service. *Tech Crunch.* Retrieved https://techcrunch.com/2019/02/11/linkedin-debuts-linkedin-live-a-new-live-video-broadcast-service/

Michaelson, L., Knight, A.B. Fink, L.D. (2004). T*eam-Based Learning: A Transformative Use of Small Groups in College Teaching.* Sterling, VA: Sylus Publishing

Moeller, S. (2019, January 3). The 2019 ultimate guide to Facebook engagement. *Buzzsumo.* Retrieved from https://buzzsumo.com/blog/facebook-engagement-guide/

Murphy, H. (2019, April 3). No, your Instagram 'influence' is not as good as cash, club owner says. *The New York Times.* Retrieved from https://www.nytimes.com/2019/04/03/world/philippines-hotel-influencers-social-media.html

Must-know influencer trends for Q1 2019: The complete report (n.d.). S*ocialbakers.* Retrieved from https://www.socialbakers.com/social-media-content/studies/must-know-influencer-trends-for-2019-the-complete-report/#modal

O'Neil, J., Moreno, Á., Rawlins, B., Valentini, C. (2018). Learning objectives:

What do students need to know and able to do for entry-level positions? In *Fast Forward Foundations and Future State. Educators and Practitioners* (pp. 45-58). New York: Commission on Public Relations Education. Retrieved from http://www.commissionpred.org/wp-content/uploads/2018/04/report6-full.pdf

Perez, S. (2018, October 30). Twitter's doubling of character count from 140 to 280 has little impact on length of tweets. Tech Crunch. Retrieved from https://techcrunch.com/2018/10/30/twitters-doubling-of-character-count-from-140-to-280-had-little-impact-on-length-of-tweets/

Quesenberry, K. A. (2015, November 18). Conducting a social media audit. *Harvard Business Review*. Retrieved from https://hbr.org/2015/11/conducting-a-social-media-audit

Quesenberry, K. A. & Coolsen, M. K. (2018). Why makes Facebook brand posts engaging? A content analysis of Facebook brand post text that increases shares, likes, and comments to influence organic viral reach. *Journal of Current Issues & Research in Advertising*. DOI: 10.1080/10641734.2018.1503113

Raji. (2019, February 11). Horizon media partners with Captiv8 to combat influencer fraud. *Captiv8*. Retrieved from https://captiv8.io/blog/2019/02/11/horizon-media-partners-with-captiv8-to-combat-influencer-fraud/

Ramdani, Z., & Taylor, E. (2018, May 10). Does social media impact SEO? We ran an experiment to find out. *Hootsuite*. Retrieved from https://blog.hootsuite.com/social-media-seo-experiment/

Rogers, E.M. (2003). *Diffusion of innovations* (5th ed.). New York, N.Y.: Free Press.

Rosenberg, E. (2019, March 22). A vegan YouTube star went to Bali. A video of her there brought her platform crashing down. *The Washington Post*. Retrieved from https://www.washingtonpost.com/technology/2019/03/22/vegan-youtube-star-rawvana-gets-caught-eating-meat-camera

Insights. (n.d.). Snapchat Support. Retrieved from https://support.snapchat.com/en-US/article/insights

Solis, B. (2012). *The rise of digital influence*. San Mateo, C.A.: Altimer Group.

The FTC's endorsement guides: What people are asking. *Federal Trade Commission*. (2017). Retrieved from https://www.ftc.gov/tips-advice/business-center/guidance/ftcs-endorsement-guides-what-people-are-asking

The global state of influencer marketing in 2019. (2019, March 18). *Talkwalker*. Retrieved from https://www.talkwalker.com/case-studies/global-state-influencer-marketing

Tigers (sports teams). (2018, December 16). *Wikipedia*. Retrieved from https://en.wikipedia.org/wiki/Tigers_(sports_teams)

Traphagen, M. (2018, November 14). Three social media strategies you can use to boost your SEO. *Search Engine Journal*. Retrieved from https://www.searchenginejournal.com/social-media-strategies-seo/277839/

Understanding breakdowns, metrics and filtering in ads reporting. *Facebook Blueprint*. Retrieved from https://www.facebook.com/business/help/264160060861852?helpref=faq_content

What is retargeting? (n.d.). *Ad Roll*. Retrieved from https://www.adroll.com/learn-more/retargeting

Whiting, A., & Williams, D. (2013). Why people use social media: A uses and gratifications approach. *Qualitative Market Research: An International Journal, 16*, 362-369.

Zarella, D. (2011). *Zarella's Hierarchy of Contagiousness: The Science, Design, and Engineering of Contagious Ideas*. USA: Do You Zoom.

Zelm, A. (2018, July 17). Facebook reach in 2018: How many fans actually see your posts? *Kuno Creative*. Retrieved from https://www.kunocreative.com/blog/facebook-reach-in-2018

ABOUT MATTHEW J. KUSHIN, PH.D.

Matthew J. Kushin, Ph.D. (@mjkushin) is an associate professor in the Department of Communication at Shepherd University. He's an award-winning educator and scholar.

At Shepherd University, Kushin developed, launched, and is the coordinator of the Strategic Communication concentration, which focuses on the intersection of public relations and social media. Classes he teaches or has taught include: Social Media, Politics & Social Media, Principles of PR, Persuasion and Message Design, Strategic Campaigns, Communication Theories, Communication Research Methods, Applied Communication Research, Communication & New Media, Writing Across Platforms, Introduction to Mass Communication, Public Speaking, New Communication Technology.

A leading voice in social media education, Kushin is the author of Social Media Syllabus (MattKushin.com), a popular blog and resource for social media educators.

Dr. Kushin is the former Director of ICBO One Global Digital Strategy for the partner organizations of the International Congress of Behavioral Optometry. He helped plan, secure sponsorship for, and launch the ICBO One social mobile app for the global behavioral optometry community. He also planned and executed the app strategy for partner events throughout the world including in Australia, Austria, Canada, Spain, the United Kingdom and the United States.

Among his many accomplishments, Kushin was the keynote speaker of the 2018 Internet Day Celebration hosted by the DigiMedia lab and the Department of Communication and Art at the University Aveiro in Portugal. He was a member of the 2019 Visiting Professors Program of the Advertising Education Foundation. He has presented his research at many national and international conferences and via the United States State Department.

Dr. Kushin's research focuses on social media, politics, and civic life.

Before joining Shepherd University in the fall of 2012, he was an assistant professor at Utah Valley University.

Learn more: http://mattkushin.com/profile/.

DOWNLOAD ASSIGNMENTS AND ACTIVITIES

Download all assignments and activities in the chapter appendices and Chapter 9 of this book in a password-protected zip file.

Use your unique password to unlock the zip file: *6022019b4$*

Download the zip file from Google Drive at:

https://drive.google.com/file/d/1zlL5PlFpXQ-RZagxkMkn0pQT5MAyp8c0/view

Or, via:

http://bit.ly/2ZBl2rp

Note: Zip files cannot be opened on most phones and tablets. Download the file to a PC or Mac, extract the files from the zipped folder, and transfer files to a smartphone or tablet for mobile access.

Printed in Great Britain
by Amazon

10223505R00132